Effective Sheltered Housing: A Handbook

Other titles in this series

Social Housing and The Social Services by Paul Spicker

Housing Finance by David Garnett, Barbara Reid and Helen Riley

Housing Practice and Information Technology by David Hunter

The Housing Service of the Future edited by David Donnison and Duncan Maclennan

Maintaining Home Ownership: The Agency Approach by Philip Leather and Sheila Mackintosh

Longman/Institute of Housing

The Housing Practice Series

EFFECTIVE SHELTERED HOUSING: A HANDBOOK

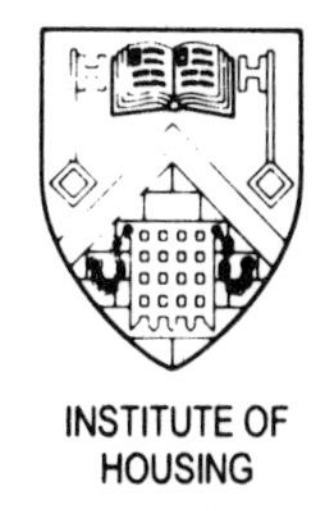

Imogen Parry and Lyn Thompson

Published by the Institute of Housing (Services) Ltd, Octavia House, Westwood Business Park, Westwood Way, Coventry CV4 8JP and Longman Group Ltd, 6th Floor, Westgate House, The High, Harlow, Essex CM20 1YR

Telephone (0279) 442601
Fax (0279) 444501

Published in the IOH/Longman Housing Practice Series under the General Editorship of Peter Williams

First Printed 1993
Reprinted 1993, August 1994.

A catalogue record for this book is available from the British Library

ISBN 0-582-09141-1

Typeset by The Midlands Book Typesetting Company, Queens Road, Loughborough, Leics. LE11 1HH
Printed in Great Britain by Antony Rowe Ltd, Chippenham, Wiltshire

Contents

Authors Acknowledgements

We would like to acknowledge and thank the hundreds of wardens with whom we have worked over the years, and who have helped to shape the ideas and views presented in this book. Indeed, the book itself is a distillation of their views and ours, and we owe each and every one of them a debt of gratitude for their contribution to discussion and debate on the myriad aspects of the rule of the warden and of sheltered housing, past present and future.

We would also like to express our gratitude to the College of North East London where we teach the Institute of Housing National Certificated Wardens Course. They have given us practical support with the production of this book, and in particular we would like to thank Jackie Pike, our Faculty Administrator, who so ably and cheerfully coped with typing and retyping our manuscript. Thanks also to Garry Saunders for his contribution on the NHS in Chapter 3 and assistance on health and safety in Chapter 7 and to Neal Purvis for his assistance with housing finance in Chapter 2.

We are grateful to: Notting Hill Housing Trust and to the residents and warden of Gloucester Court, North Kensington for enabling the cover photographs to be taken; Becci Thompson for taking the photographs and Rod Tubbs for the cover design.

Finally, we would like to say thank you to our families for their invaluable patience and support throughout this project.

Imogen Parry & Lyn Thompson

November 1992

Parry Thompson Associates

The authors have worked together for a number of years in two complementary capacities. Firstly as half time lecturers and co-tutors on the National Wardens Certificated Course at the College of North East London and secondly as freelance consultants and trainers, specialising in the design and delivery of short and long training courses in community care, communication and management skills for local authorities and housing associations.

Readers wishing to discuss wardens' or other groups of workers' training needs with the authors are invited to contact us at the address at the back of this book, listed under Parry Thompson Associates.

England

The authors wish to point out to readers that our work experience has been in England and therefore this book is aimed primarily at wardens working in that country. However, much of what we say applies to those employed in Wales, Scotland and Northern Ireland too.

Introduction

Sheltered housing is at a crossroads. The expansion of Community Care, the increasing frail elderly population, together with major changes in the way social housing is provided and managed, are dramatically affecting the role and function both of sheltered housing and of wardens.

This book is intended to help wardens meet this challenge effectively.

Wardens will play a crucial role in ensuring the success of sheltered housing in the future – the manner in which it meets changing needs in an ever more demanding environment. We firmly believe that wardens, a traditionally undervalued set of workers, are a highly motivated and professional group who have long deserved proper recognition and a consequent improvement in status. We hope that this book will contribute to discussion and debate on this issue, leading to the ultimate empowerment of wardens themselves and the older people with whom they work.

The subject matter covered by this book is based around the syllabus for the Institute of Housing's one year national Certificated Wardens Course, and the book will be of particular interest and value to students studying for, or intending to take, this course. However, the range of issues covered by the book are workplace-focused and will therefore be of relevance to all wardens and their managers, regardless of their access to training and education.

The book is aimed towards all those who work with older people in sheltered housing, grouped housing schemes or designated flats, bungalow or houses in the public, voluntary or private sectors and their managers. In other words, everyone for whom the title 'warden' might be appropriate, although in practice you might be called something different, such as Resident Estate Manager, Estate Welfare Worker or Sheltered Housing Officer. These, together with Resident, Deputy, Mobile, Visiting, Relief, Neighbourhood and Assistant Warden are just some of the range of the titles the authors have encountered. For the sake of convenience we use the general title 'Warden' throughout the book.

The issues covered by the book are divided into two parts. The first consists of an examination of the context of the wardens job, including the organisation of services, the policies which lie behind service provision and the way in which these affect current and future working practices.

The second part of the book considers in depth the skills and techniques practised by the warden as communicator, manager and specialist worker with older people.

The authors were formerly a social worker and a wardens' manager respectively before jointly tutoring the National Certificated Wardens Course at the College of North East London for the past six years. We have therefore been privileged to work with a wide range of wardens from London boroughs, district councils, housing associations and the private sector over the years. The ideas expressed throughout this book are distilled from the experiences, perceptions and views of the many wardens we have known, combined with views and ideas of our own. The book is unique in that it reports for the first time such a range of hitherto unrecorded knowledge and ideas, and in presenting and examining in depth a wide range of practice issues for wardens.

We hope the book will encourage wardens to recognise, evaluate and enhance the range of skills they practice, together with developing the knowledge they need to carry out their demanding jobs. The book does not attempt to lay down the law, or to assert that there is only one way to run sheltered housing. Instead, we hope it will be seen as a resource which will stimulate thought and discussion, enabling wardens themselves, in conjunction with their managers, to formulate a range of solutions appropriate to the challenges they face.

PART 1
The historical, policy and organisational context of sheltered housing

CHAPTER 1 The role of the warden

Introduction

The development of the role of the warden and that of sheltered housing itself are inextricably linked, and we therefore consider them together in this chapter. Taking an overview of the major influences on the warden's role, we consider how it has evolved from the notion of a good neighbour to that of today's front-line manager of care services for older people.

In the first part of this chapter we consider the evolution of sheltered housing itself and how there has been little or no thought-out policy planning for this provision; such legislation as there is has often regulated existing practice, rather than initiated new policies. We examine how the role of the warden has also developed in a similarly *ad hoc* fashion, and we look at how this lack of clarity has led to much confusion surrounding the warden's job. Indeed, one of the most striking issues affecting the role of the warden is just how many different perceptions exist about who the warden is, what he or she can be expected to do – or not do – and how it should be done. Many of you reading this will have direct experience of working within such confusion, and will know how difficult your job can be as a result.

We touch on how the demographic changes leading to greater numbers of older, frailer elderly people continue to affect the role of the warden, and on some of the practical dilemmas wardens face as a result. Demography itself is looked at in greater depth in Chapter 3.

We describe the history and development of central control alarm systems in depth and evaluate their influence over the changing role of the warden.

In the second part of this chapter, we look at current issues affecting the role of the warden. We focus on the isolated nature of the job itself, combined as it so frequently is with little or no training and a lack of clear understanding of the role by management, tenants and other professionals. We consider how this presents unique difficulties to wardens, and we shall attempt to formulate some solutions.

Finally, having taken a look at the current and possible future influences on the role of the warden, we appraise the need for a realistic warden-focused re-definition of the purpose and function of the job, to take account of the demands and needs of our client group towards and beyond the year 2000.

Historical Influences on the Role of the Warden

Provision for Increasing Numbers of Older People

The first of the major factors which have significantly affected the role of the warden and its development could be said to be the increase in the elderly population this century, combined with a decline of the role of the family in providing care, support and accommodation for their elders. Paradoxically, however, more recent government care in the community policies have begun to reverse this trend, encouraging the family to provide care previously expected from the state, whilst stimulating greater involvement from the private sector. The burden of such caring, particularly in the 1960s, 1970s and 1980s, fell upon the state, either through local authorities or voluntary organisations. Such provision can roughly be divided into long-term hospital care, residential care, and sheltered housing.

Care in the community policies have meant that long-term hospital care provision has declined significantly in recent years. However, whilst little new public sector residential care is being provided now, it still remains a significant aspect of long-term care for older people. Set up under Part 3 of the 1948 National Assistance Act, such provision is often referred to as 'Old People's Homes', 'Residential Homes for the Elderly', or, more colloquially, simply as 'Part 3'. At the time of writing (1992) Part 3 accommodation is administered and managed directly by local authority Social Services Departments, although the full implementation of care in the community policies (see Chapter 3) will lead to 'arms length' management and a significant decline in the direct provision of Part 3 by Local Authorities. There has been an explosion in the number of privately run residential homes for the older people.

But we are concerned here with the third form of provision, sheltered housing which, whilst housing proportionally fewer older people than Part 3 provision nevertheless provides a significant contribution towards providing support – and, more latterly – care for the elderly. The greatest proportion of sheltered housing schemes have been, and continue to be, developed, built and managed by organisations concerned with housing, whether local authority housing departments, private building companies or housing associations, including almshouses (although a few are managed by social services). Wardens are some of the very few employees of such organisations who actually may provide 'hands-on' care – and they may well be managed by housing officers having little or no understanding of the role of the warden, the remit of sheltered housing and the needs of the elderly. There are, of course, some shining examples of exceptions to this rule, but a general impression we have gained from our work with a number of wardens is that the role of the warden is unlikely to be clearly defined and understood by employers.

The development of sheltered housing

The evolution of sheltered housing is the second major factor that could be said to have influenced the way the wardens job has evolved. There is a temptation to perceive sheltered housing as a modern concept, but we must not forget that almshouses have existed since the tenth century and it could be argued that they are the model upon which the concept of sheltered housing is based. Many of you reading this may be working in almshouses today, set up with funds from philanthropic bequests or charities to provide supported housing for the 'poor elderly' of a particular district. Others of you may be working in schemes which are based architecturally, if not financially, on such a model.

Origins of the title 'Sheltered Housing'

The origin of the title 'sheltered' housing is somewhat unclear. The 1944 Ministry of Health Housing Manual discusses the need for choosing a 'sheltered site' when building housing specifically intended for elderly people, by which they presumably meant sheltered from wind, snow and driving rain. As time has passed the concept of sheltering from the weather has grown and changed to encompass the concept of being both protected and looked after in all aspects of life once the move to such housing has been made. It could be argued here that this is a somewhat false premise upon which to base a move from the tenant's point of view, given that the wardens' role is to enable the tenant to live an independent life – perhaps this is part of the explanation for the confusion surrounding the role of the warden.

'*The Last Refuge*'

A major influence on the development of sheltered housing has been Peter Townsend's book *The Last Refuge*, published in 1962. This was a wide-ranging study of the residential (Part 3) sector of institutional care, in which he concluded that residents had a very low quality of life, being subjected to routines and regimentation which suited the staff rather than met residents' needs and were given little, if any, mental stimulation. Yet residents were not all so physically or mentally frail that they needed the care input that was available, being able in many cases to do much more for themselves than they were given the opportunity to do. Townsend's view was that, for many residents, there should be far greater provision of specifically designed and built accommodation to enable older people to lead independent lives within the community. Indeed, he suggested that for every 1000 of the population over 65 years of age, 50 sheltered dwellings should be provided. One of the models on which Townsend had based his ideas had been a bungalow development in rural Devon, built in 1948, where residents were linked to their resident warden by a bell which they could activate to let the warden know when they needed assistance.

The impact of the views expressed by Townsend gave publicity to the need for an increase in the provision of sheltered housing.

Townsend's observations on the way in which the over-protective and regimented caring practices in Part 3 homes removed autonomy and self-determination from clients are in sharp contrast to the idea of sheltered housing, and the role of the warden as enabler, assisting the independence of tenants leading their own lives. This concept has continued to have a wide impact upon the role of the warden, although in order for the warden to carry out this function satisfactorily, the tenants concerned must of course, have some degree of independence to assist. Later in this chapter we will discuss the dilemma facing wardens through the impact of the increasingly ageing population upon allocations to sheltered housing, resulting in large numbers of frail and dependent elderly becoming tenants.

Categories 1 and 2

The next identifiable stage in the development of sheltered housing also gave us the colloquial phrases by which different types of sheltered housing are still known, 'Category 1' and 'Category 2'. These were described in a Ministry of Housing and Local Government Circular *Housing Standard and Costs; accommodation specially designed for Old People* (Circular 82/69 1969). It spoke of the need to provide housing to maintain the independence of the elderly, and divided the two types of developments for which central government funding support would be available into Category 1 (for the fitter, more active elderly) and Category 2 (for the frailer elderly). The circular laid down minimum design standards for sheltered housing schemes. Prior to this, the design and building of such housing had varied widely from authority to authority in terms of size, numbers of dwellings, availability of facilities etc, but from the early 1970s to the early 1980s, the majority of sheltered schemes built by Housing Associations and Local Authorities throughout the country followed the guidelines prescribed by this circular.

Category 1 schemes were perceived as being intended for the younger, fitter, more active elderly, some of whom might be couples. Category 2 schemes were for the less mobile, older (but still independent) elderly.

There was to be a clear distinction between the design of each type of scheme. Category 1 schemes (where the site allowed) were often built as separate blocks of dwellings, grouped around gardens and/or a common room, with Category 2 schemes consisting of a large single block with all flats and facilities connected by lifts and heated corridors. However, the principle of dividing elderly people in this way for the purposes of allocations and management has, as wardens know only too well, largely been found to be impractical. The younger, fitter elderly allocated flats in Category 1 schemes eventually become older and frailer; however, unless a transfer is requested by tenants themselves, there cannot be any imposed 'moving on' between schemes. And again, as wardens know to their cost, to have an entire scheme full of very frail elderly people imposes an intolerable burden on the warden, which can only be eased by a balanced allocations policy coupled with adequate domiciliary services and support to the frailest residents.

Whilst Circular 82/69 is no longer mandatory upon public sector providers of sheltered housing, it exerted a very strong influence over the way schemes were conceived and built for over ten years. The circular's recommended ratio of tenants to warden of 30 flats (but possibly more tenants as some might be couples) to one warden by local authorities, was viewed as a bench mark by policy makers, rather as was Townsend's recommended ratio of 50 sheltered dwellings per thousand elderly people some years earlier. Given that the peak period for building sheltered housing took place throughout the mid 1970s and early 1980s, large numbers of wardens are working in schemes built following the precepts of this circular.

As the bricks and mortar side of the sheltered housing developed and evolved, so did the role of the warden, with a number of strands coming together to create the multi-faceted aspects of the job as it is carried out today.

Good Neighbour Schemes

Alongside the building of dwellings specifically intended for the elderly, with perhaps a nearby flat or house designated for the warden, there existed a number of *ad hoc* good neighbour schemes developing in various areas across the country. It can be contended that these schemes played a part in shaping the role of the warden. In many cases such schemes came into being following the identification of a number of isolated older people living in tower blocks or flatted estates, built as a result of slum clearance programmes in the 1950s and early 1960s. The destruction of local neighbourhoods with younger families perhaps moving out to the new towns in search of work and new opportunities, meant that many elderly people were left without family, neighbourhood or community support. One response to this was to recruit a local person – most frequently a woman, whose children had perhaps grown up or at least were at school – to act literally as a 'good neighbour', and to knock on the doors of designated older people, offering to collect pensions or shopping, or offer other similar assistance to that which might previously have been available informally through family or local networks.

Often such schemes were set up in response to publicly expressed concern about the numbers of isolated elderly people living in a particular area, sometimes following newspaper stories of an elderly person lying dead and undiscovered in their flat for days or weeks because no one knew they were there or was prepared to take responsibility for them. Usually the 'good neighbour' was recruited on a semi-voluntary basis, being paid a small wage, or expenses only; the scheme may have been initiated by a local authority, whether a Housing Department or Social Services Department, or perhaps through a local voluntary organisation.

In rural areas, similar initiatives were also developing to support and assist isolated elderly people. Although such schemes, whether metropolitan or rural, were not great in number, they nevertheless brought into focus the need for supporting older people with their independence – and the concept of the 'good neighbour' which they encompassed was for many years a fundamental aspect of the role of all wardens, whether resident, visiting, deputy, or relief. Indeed, although increasing pressures mean that it is an outdated concept, many wardens' employers continue to use the phrase in job specifications. Many schemes such as the ones described above still exist today, perhaps with the original good neighbour role strengthened and enhanced, maybe also employing alarm system technology; but the basic principle of supporting the elderly to maintain their independence in their own homes continues to be a cornerstone of the warden's work.

The principle of the warden as 'good neighbour' however, presents more difficulties now that increasingly physically and mentally frail residents are moving into sheltered housing, making far more demands upon the warden than even the most altruistic good neighbour could be expected to meet.

The perception of warden as 'good neighbour' has proved increasingly problematic over the years. The lack of regard in which the job has been held by other professionals – not only social workers, district nurses and GPs for example, but also more significantly, many wardens' employers themselves – is in part a reflection of the way the job is conceived of by others.

This, in turn, could be one of the reasons why few training opportunities existed for wardens until relatively recently – why should a neighbour need training to carry out tasks for which, after all, only common sense should be necessary? We return to the themes of training and education later in this chapter. What is becoming clear is that the original role of the warden as traditionally perceived has rapidly become obsolete as demands on skills and knowledge have increased.

Extra-Care Sheltered Housing

A further landmark in the development of sheltered housing was the increased prominence that 'Extra Care' or 'Very Sheltered Housing' schemes gained in the late 1970s and early 1980s. Such schemes were a response to the perceived drift towards frailty within existing sheltered housing, creating demands for hands-on care which the warden alone could not reasonably be expected to provide. Whilst the role of wardens working within such schemes is different from, and in many cases, clearer than that of other wardens, the overall influence of such schemes on the wardens' role and on the way sheltered housing has since developed is questionable.

In general, such schemes have been built (or converted) by housing organisations but receive some funding or staffing facilities from either Social Services or Health Authorities or, in some cases, both. The warden is normally perceived as the organiser of the care services provided. Extra physical provision available may include communal dining rooms, a nursing annexe, and specifically designed or adapted bathrooms; the enhanced staffing arrangements may include care assistants, extra provision of home help or home care staff, regular visits from district nurses, and a rota system of wardens to ensure on-the-spot 24-hour cover.

The phrases used to describe the provision therefore imply a kind of half-way house between sheltered housing and Part 3 accommodation, and many of those who embraced the concept initially perceived it as the answer to the problem of increasing levels of frailty within sheltered housing.

A widely publicised initiative by Warwickshire Social Services Department in the mid-1970s raised the profile of such schemes and also pointed to the necessity for collaboration between all the providers of services for older people in order for such schemes to be successful. It is this latter aspect of Extra Care Sheltered Housing which has had the most lasting influence.

The concept of extra care sheltered housing has been the subject of much debate since its inception. Those in favour claimed initially that it would solve the problem of how to help those very frail elderly people who could no longer manage in traditional sheltered housing. However, this implied that there would be some imposed 'moving-on' which is both unacceptable and impractical. Therefore, extra care housing has never been able to solve the problem of sheltered housing schemes with an existing high level of frailty since such tenants would be unlikely to choose to move. It can therefore only offer places to those on the waiting list who are perceived to be too frail for Category 1 or 2 sheltered schemes, and who might otherwise have been admitted to Part 3 homes.

There are also those who question whether it is appropriate for housing organisations to be providing such a high level of personal care, either because they consider this to be more appropriately the role of the social services, or because it seems to provide 'so much for so few' – a criticism also aimed at sheltered housing in general.

It has, however, provided some exemplary models of collaborative working practices between the providers of care for older people. Those who were not in favour of diverting limited capital resources towards the building of such schemes often supported the argument that a more flexible attitude towards the provision of support to existing frail tenants of Category 1 & 2 sheltered schemes would be a more appropriate use of energy and funding.

Interestingly, although the concept as originally envisaged in the 1970s was not adopted in a wholesale fashion by large numbers of local authorities and housing associations, the co-operation between health, housing and social services departments which developed is now endorsed by current community care initiatives, which we discuss in Chapter 3.

Because the debate surrounding the Extra-care approach is so topical for wardens coping with the very frail elderly we find that many students choose to investigate this area during their studies for the National Certificated Wardens Course. Their observations, not surprisingly, endorse the value of close co-operation between all those providing care services for the elderly, whilst also calling into question, in many cases, the definition of 'frail elderly' used when allocating places in such schemes. We have read numbers of reports where wardens compare the levels of frailty they find on Extra-care schemes with those on their own Category 1 or 2 schemes, and find that, paradoxically, the tenants of the schemes visited seem in many cases fitter and more independent than their own!

This does not, of course, detract from the value of such schemes to the frail elderly who live there, many of whom are being enabled to remain in their own homes with all the necessary care and support coming to them, rather than having to move on because Category 1 or 2 sheltered housing is no longer appropriate. However, wardens who carry out these visits generally tend to conclude that the value of the scheme lies in the care provision which comes out of the enhanced staffing structure and co-operative working practices, rather than in the building itself; and that this is the element of Extra-care housing which would benefit frail tenants on their own schemes if such a model were to be universally adopted.

Because such schemes came about through perceived need, and without specific legislation to determine either the built form or the client group, the colloquial titles 'Extra Care' or 'Very Sheltered Housing' are reasonably accurate descriptions.

'Category two and a half' implies something between Category 2 Sheltered Housing, (which, as we have seen, is intended for the frailer elderly yet with some degree of independence) and Part III accommodation, set up under Part III of the 1948 National Assistance Act for those who clearly cannot manage to live in their own homes any longer. As a colloquial title for the provision, Category two and a half is frequently used. However, in the interests of accuracy, it must be remembered that such a category does not exist officially, in the ways that Category 1 and Category 2 sheltered housing do. It is equally inaccurate to refer to such provision as 'Part two and a half' for the same reason.

The Development of Alarm Systems

The increasing sophistication of the alarm systems available to local authorities from the early 1980s not only had a significant effect upon the role of the warden but the introduction of central control systems also meant sweeping changes in the conditions of service and methods of working for many wardens.

In order to put this into context, it is helpful to consider the history of alarm systems, which have always been one of the traditional 'tools of the trade' for wardens.

Early Systems

The very first systems may even have been, in some cases, more basic than the one Townsend observed in the 1948 Devon development, which had a bell activated by the tenant which rang in the warden's house or flat. Some did not even have this facility, simply ringing loudly somewhere outside, making sufficient noise in many cases to alert not only the warden but also all the other tenants and wider neighbourhood. Clumsy and primitive though these systems were, they did have the advantage of encouraging neighbours to take responsibility for each other, especially in the warden's absence, for at this time there were few organised relief warden systems.

One major disadvantage of such systems was their advertisement to the world at large of the presence of a vulnerable elderly person, giving an opportunity that unscrupulous burglars and conmen at times found hard to resist. Perhaps more significant from the wardens' point of view, was the fact that every single alarm call had to be actioned by going to the flat from which it originated, false alarm or not, middle of the night notwithstanding.

Two-way Speech Systems

The development of two-way speech systems where the warden could speak to the tenant from a control board located in his or her flat or office meant that the all-important reassurance that help was on its way could be given to a tenant in difficulties, whilst false alarms could be dealt with, in most cases, without having to go to the flat of the resident concerned. It is interesting to conjecture at this point how far such systems affected the way in which wardens carried out their everyday work; wardens who previously had physically visited each resident on their scheme each day that they were on duty had an opportunity to sit in their flat or office and call up each person on the intercom. This aspect of the work of the warden often arouses heated debate, since there are those for whom it is normal practice – indeed, a requirement of their employer – to call up each resident every day still, the only exceptions being residents who have specifically requested not to be called. On the other hand there are wardens who view this as an intolerable invasion of tenants' privacy, preferring to ensure the well-being of each of their residents by far less obtrusive methods, which often include supporting or helping to form a neighbourhood network, and only visiting when requested to do so. No doubt this debate will continue to rage for years to come, long after the alarm systems which may have initiated it become obsolete.

Such systems as described were all that was available in the early years of sheltered housing. By the mid-1970s a somewhat more sophisticated speech system was on the market, where a warden could take a small portable receiver throughout the scheme and plug it in wherever there was an intercom point, whether the warden's own flat, office, common room or another resident's flat. This had the obvious advantage of easing communication, and allowing a warden to spend as long as was needed in an individual's flat, for example, knowing they could be contacted if necessary from elsewhere on the scheme. A somewhat subtle, but nevertheless significant, disadvantage of this system was the idea that the more easily the warden could be contacted, the less motivation there tended to be for tenants to take responsibility for each other's well being.

Providing Cover for the Warden

Alongside the development of these relatively simple technical methods of bringing assistance to sheltered tenants grew the gradual awareness of the need to regularise the resident warden's hours of duty, to define how much cover sheltered housing tenants should expect, and to clarify exactly who was responsible for answering alarm calls in the warden's absence.

A number of management issues needed to be resolved. Given that the warden generally lived on site, it was expected that he or she would answer alarm calls not only during hours of duty but during time off also, if she or he happened to be at home. This not only created ambiguity with regard to expectations of the wardens by management and tenants, it also meant that in practice many wardens felt guilty about going out shopping or spending an evening out – they would never forgive themselves should an emergency occur which they were not there to deal with, however legitimate their absence.

Relief Warden Services

A variety of systems were employed by authorities to provide cover for the warden over longer periods of absence, such as annual leave, or sickness. Some organisations provided relief wardens who would cover for a designated period, perhaps even sleeping over in the guest room, if there was one. Sometimes this worked well, at others it was less satisfactory. One reason for this was that many relief wardens had to gain access to the alarm systems through the wardens flat, or even sleep in the resident wardens flat should there be no guest room, meaning a complete invasion of privacy for the poor resident warden.

Employing relief wardens was also perceived as expensive and cumbersome by employers, since only one scheme could be covered at a time and there was no flexibility to allow one warden to be off duty, another off sick and another on holiday, for example, without paying three extra lots of wages in addition to those of the resident staff. Although this had disadvantages, it was perhaps more popular with wardens than some alternatives, such as having their cleaner deputise for them, or relying on unknown agency staff.

Another widely used, although controversial, method of providing relief cover was that of the designated 'responsible tenant'. This is another issue which causes heated debate when discussed, for there are those whose view it is that anyone who needs sheltered housing, for whatever reason, should not be placed in a position to take over responsibility for the health and welfare of all the other tenants in the warden's absence. In addition, it raises issues of confidentiality, and either possible or actual access to records of fellow-tenants. The opposing view is that it is an ageist concept to consider that, simply because someone lives in sheltered housing they are not able or capable of providing assistance to their neighbours when needed, or being responsible for areas such as security of buildings etc. There are also those who view it as obtaining cover 'on the cheap' by management.

Such methods of cover as described could never give the comprehensive 24-hour cover provided by the warden when on duty or on the scheme, at least – and they did nothing to address the ambiguity over what the wardens actual hours of duty and responsibilities really were. In addition, they tended to raise questions in the minds of tenants and their relatives about the level of cover that could be expected. One ultimate outcome of this lack of clarity was that many wardens felt both guilty and trapped, rarely leaving their schemes and regularly working over and above their weekly designated hours. All this may well have been compounded by the fact that wardens were a somewhat isolated and unsupported group, not regarded as part of the organisational structure of their employing authority and with few opportunities to express their views and feelings to management.

24-Hour Central Control Systems

Once the technology became available to centralise all calls from a group of sheltered housing schemes to one central point, thus ensuring that every sheltered housing tenant in a particular authority had emergency cover whether the warden was there or not, it seemed that salvation for wardens and their managers had arrived.

The Earliest Systems

Initially, this equipment was somewhat primitive by comparison with the advanced technology with which many wardens are familiar today. One of the earliest two-way speech systems between a number of sheltered housing locations and a central point where calls could be answered, was developed by a company then called Davis Safety Controls (now Davis Communications) in conjunction with a company called 'Dynamic Logic'. Davis had a number of fixed-link alarm systems operating in sheltered housing schemes in the London Borough of Hammersmith and Fulham. Initially, the idea was to link their systems from one sheltered scheme to another to enable one warden to cover two, or even three schemes whose own warden was away or off sick, using the warden's own alarm system to speak to the tenant, ascertain the problem, give comfort and reassurance where necessary, and to call on a peripatetic warden based at the Housing Office to visit the tenant where necessary.

From this very simple beginning, developed by Davis to meet the Borough's specific needs at the time (1978) grew the idea of centralising all calls from every sheltered scheme in the Borough to one point, operated by staff trained in dealing with older people, and with a mobile warden always on duty to go out in a specially equipped van to deal with any emergency occurring during resident wardens' off duty hours, annual leave, sickness and even when schemes had no warden, pending recruitment. Key issues for the Borough of Hammersmith and Fulham in implementing the system were proper training for control centre operators and mobile wardens, and as much opportunity as possible for these staff members to liaise with all Borough's Resident Wardens and to spend time on the schemes they covered, getting to know the residents so that they were not strangers when they answered emergency calls.

The system was up and running in Hammersmith and Fulham by 1979, and despite some technical hiccups, was an enormous success. The implementation of the system is described in detail in 'The Role of central control in dispersed alarm systems' (Thompson 1980) in Butler and Oldman's *Alarm Systems for the Elderly: Report of a Workshop* (1980) which also looks at a number of further early alarm system initiatives across the country. The system created a great deal of interest amongst other authorities looking to solve their sheltered housing management problems, and the tiny office in which the control centre was based was often too small for the groups of councillors and officers from across the country who came to look at the new technology and discuss the management philosophy.

The Growth of Central Control Systems

Other alarm system manufacturers soon realised that this was where the future lay. As is often the case with pioneering prototypes, the technology developed subsequently by others was more sophisticated and streamlined than the original version, which is perhaps why, although Davis were the first, the number of their installations is now outweighed across the country by those of other manufacturers.

Certainly, such a system created freedom previously undreamed of for resident wardens. They could work a 5 day week, with evenings and nights off; they could attend training courses and wardens meetings, they could go away on holiday without feeling guilty, and all this whilst knowing that their scheme was being covered for emergencies by a properly trained member of staff whom they knew and trusted. It seemed to combine the positive aspects of the bad old days whilst eliminating their problems, and pointed to a brighter future. Indeed, the wholesale adoption of such schemes by large numbers of authorities across the country during the following twelve years has made a major contribution towards improving the working conditions of many wardens, not to mention the comfort and security it has brought to countless residents of sheltered housing, and, more latterly, to older people living on their own in the wider community also.

The Positive Benefits of Central Control Systems

We are concerned here, of course, with the influences on the role of the warden this development has had. On the positive side, as well as the freedom from guilt that has been possible, wardens now have a greater physical freedom to leave their schemes. In some areas this has enabled wardens to carry out aspects of their work with older people living in the wider community, to spread some of the benefits of sheltered housing a little more widely. This was one of the fundamental precepts of the Hammersmith and Fulham warden management philosophy; sheltered housing could be regarded as a provision for a minority of the privileged elite, yet there were many more isolated older people who now could be drawn into the social life of the sheltered scheme, and receive support from the warden. In this way sheltered housing could be regarded as a community facility, a focal point for elderly people living in a particular area, and of benefit to a far wider group of people than simply the 40 or so residents. The introduction of a central control alarm system in the borough enabled this philosophy to be put into practice, and it influenced other authorities to consider it positively in this way also.

The Negative Aspects of Central Control Systems

On the negative side, however, it created other more sinister possibilities, which need to be considered alongside its evident advantages.

There was from the beginning, it seemed, a wholesale and unquestioning acceptance of the whole technological approach to solving management problems. Manufacturers brought out glossy literature showing shining pieces of equipment alongside stereotypical pictures of older people pulling alarm cords with (usually female) wardens arriving in the nick of time to save them from some unspecified fate. A subliminal message accompanied this literature – install the right technology and make everyone happy. However, other messages came across also – the elderly as being dependent, the wardens as the focus of that dependence, the need to ensure, through technology, that at all times sheltered housing tenants had round the clock protection, thus raising the expectations of those receiving the service. A subtle shift began to occur in people's perception of sheltered housing, which perhaps created even more confusion as to the role of the warden. We were seeing two perspectives on sheltered housing at the same time – that of the provision of accommodation designed to enable the elderly to lead independent lives within the community juxtaposed with the image of a 24-hour, 7-day, year-round protected environment for vulnerable elderly people.

Further problems included the perception, by some groups at least, that since sheltered tenants already had so much support, services such as Meals on Wheels or Home Help support, already spread thinly and suffering from the many cutbacks which took place during the 1980s, might be better targetted towards older people living in the community, rather than in what they saw as the somewhat over privileged environment of the sheltered housing scheme.

The most threatening possibility of all surrounding the introduction of centralised mobile relief warden systems was the opportunity it offered to authorities wanting to save money to dispense with resident wardens altogether. After all, if the whole of one borough or district could be covered for emergencies through the judicious use of technology combined with a rota of control operators and mobile wardens, why pay for a resident warden at each scheme? Luckily this breathtakingly short-sighted policy, showing a grievous lack of understanding of the warden's role other than simply dealing with emergencies, was actually put into practice by very few organisations. It was, however – and continues to be – a threat to the role of the resident warden.

Another aspect of the installation of such systems that wardens have frequently raised, whilst admitting it is difficult to prove or quantify, is the feeling that they have contributed to a further decline in tenants' willingness to be neighbourly towards one another. No longer need they rally round in the absence of the warden, since at the touch of a button, or pull of a cord, problems will be dealt with by the mobile warden. Similarly, they suggest, families may feel that their relatives are now given such comprehensive 24-hour care by the warden plus the central control back up service that they can take less responsibility themselves. The resident warden has to work very hard, therefore, to redress this balance and to re-educate everyone as to what sheltered housing is really about.

Studies have shown (e.g. Clapham and Munro 1988; Butler 1989) that the value of alarm systems as perceived by tenants are relatively low, and considerably less significant than the value of the accommodation they occupy. Furthermore, we must consider, especially with respect to dispersed alarms, the feelings and choices of the older person concerned. Malcolm Fisk (1989) argues that by allowing the spread of alarm devices, we might be threatening to undermine the self esteem of elderly people. Alan Butler was sounding a warning note regarding the wholesale and unquestioning adoption of such systems as far back as 1980 (*ibid.*).

Wardens still operating simple, old fashioned alarm systems, or those without access to central control cover may feel hard done by when they compare themselves with their large numbers of colleagues who have access to more sophisticated technology but although as we have seen here the effects on the role of the warden have been far reaching and largely positive, there are also some insidious disadvantages, which must be considered in order to reach a truly balanced perspective.

Current issues affecting the role of the warden

Introduction

Having evaluated the historical influences and factors which have contributed towards shaping the wardens' role, we shall now consider some current issues problems and dilemmas affecting wardens and the way they work, including the increasing fraility of tenants, the lack of proper management support and the isolation experienced by many wardens in carrying out this demanding job. Alongside this, we consider how training and education, together with a re-definition of the warden's role and a recognition of the warden as a professional can provide a way forward.

Increasingly Frail Tenants

Many employers seem to be reluctant to face the paradox presented by the fundamental precept of the wardens' job – to provide only as much support as is necessary to enable tenants to remain independent. Whilst this quite rightly continues to apply to those tenants who still maintain some degree of independence, such tenants are, as wardens know only too well, becoming fewer and fewer. Instead, allocations are frequently made to frail and dependent elderly people, some of whom may even have been refused a place in Part 3 accommodation. The original aim and purpose of the warden's job is therefore becoming incompatible with the client group now being serviced, and it could even be argued that sheltered housing provision is drifting towards the residential care that it was designed to replace. Some authorities, recognising this drift some years ago set up Extra Care Sheltered Schemes in an attempt to address this problem, as we have seen earlier in this chapter.

The Lack of Management Support for Wardens

This disparity between the aims of sheltered housing and the increasing fraility of its tenants raises a number of management issues which must be addressed. The warden cannot, single handedly, perform a caring role for large numbers of frail older people; support services such as home carers, district nurses and domestic staff must be available, needing co-operation and liaison between housing, social services and health authorities at every level.

However, for those wardens grappling largely unsupported with an increasingly physically and mentally frail client group, there may be a need to clearly and continuously express to management the levels of fraility and demands upon the scheme. These issues are taken up in Chapters 4 and 7.

Earlier in this chapter we looked briefly at the lack of support, communication and supervision many wardens receive from their line managers, and at the general lack of understanding of the role of the warden which seems to be fairly common. Indeed, this is a theme to which we return at various points throughout the book. This is not always the fault of the line manager, who may perhaps be a housing officer with a number of other conflicting responsibilities or demands on their time. The impetus to properly support, communicate with and supervise wardens must be present at a high level within the organisation. There are some shining examples of good practice in some local authorities and housing associations, of course, usually where responsibility for the sheltered housing service lies with one officer or a particular section, having a clear knowledge and understanding of this particular form of provision and a genuine understanding of the warden's role. But sadly these seem few and far between, and the general lack of clear direction and management of wardens only serves to increase the lack of clarity surrounding the wardens' role.

Policies and practices of the wider organisation must consider provision for the elderly in its widest context, and should involve wardens at policy formulating level, whilst offering the necessary support to enable the day-to-day work to be carried out satisfactorily and problems to be recognised and tackled. Chapter 7 discusses in greater depth the relationship between wardens and their managers, and Chapter 4 looks at, amongst other areas, assertiveness skills and report writing, both of which may need to be utilised when bringing difficult or contentious issues to the attention of managers and making recommendations towards policy formulation.

Wardens' Isolation

Many wardens are extremely isolated. Although surrounded by tenants, they have little contact with their peers. It is generally recognised to be beneficial for all workers to have an identified set of colleagues with whom they can informally and easily share problems, and discuss issues. It is difficult, especially at the beginning of a new job, to assess how well we are doing, indeed whether we are approaching the work correctly at all. We often use our colleagues as an informal sounding board to discuss criteria against which we can measure our own job performance, but this is rarely available to wardens, contributing further to their isolation.

The problem of isolation is further compounded by the aspect of living on the job or 'living in a goldfish bowl' as many wardens have described it. For resident wardens, not only is their private life on permanent display to their tenants – the identity of their visitors, what time they arrive – or go home – what their children are doing and so on – but there is never any escape from the situation, since home is work and work is home. There are, of course, advantages to living on the job which wardens would be the first to defend – no travelling to work and subsidised accommodation are two examples – but these advantages have their down side, in that there is little opportunity to get away from work, and moving up the ladder of promotion is difficult, if not impossible, when tied accommodation is a factor.

The Need for Clear Boundaries

The combination of isolation, lack of regular communication with peers and colleagues, and little opportunity to escape from the workplace can mean that wardens find it hard to set clear boundaries for themselves. As a result wardens often find themselves pulled in a number of conflicting directions through the demands of tenants, tenants' relatives, and other professionals, such as social workers, GPs, District Nurses, Home Helps – each of whom has a different concept of the warden's role, and a set of expectations and demands to match that concept. Wardens themselves may be very clear that despite others' expectations the role continues to be to maintain the independence of the elderly. Many of the assumptions made about the role by others who come into contact with wardens, however, mean that inappropriate tasks are expected of them, some of which may undermine the independence of the tenants, and some of which may compensate for the under provision of services to the elderly. Wardens can thus fall into a trap which we call the 'TWIT' syndrome – 'The Warden Is There'. The underlying theme of this assumption is, of course, that because 'The Warden Is There', relatives can offload their responsibilities, hospitals can discharge elderly patients too early into the care of the warden, and social workers are reluctant to take elderly clients from sheltered housing onto their caseload because, after all, 'The Warden Is There'.

Clearly, this places wardens in a dilemma for which there is no simple solution. In the short term, saying 'no' to such demands, whilst perhaps the most correct option would create extreme problems and possibly hardship for the tenant concerned, which wardens would find unacceptable. Saying 'yes' to the demands, however, creates a long term problem for wardens themselves, since even greater assumptions then tend to be made about how much work the warden is prepared to take on – and how much less everyone else has to do as a result. It seems that a recognised re-definition of the role of the wardens and its boundaries may be the only long-term solution.

Training and Education

The important place that training and education can have in enabling wardens to address the issues and dilemmas we have considered has only relatively recently been recognised. Adequate training for sheltered housing staff has been sadly lacking over the years, perhaps again due to the unclear nature of the role.

Induction training is vital to ensure that the warden understands the employing organisation and their own role within it – after all, they are the most frequently encountered representatives of that organisation from their tenant's point of view. Induction training also ensures that the warden understands the basics of the job; ongoing workplace-based training gives the opportunity not only to learn and understand more about practical issues and interpersonal skills but to meet with others doing similar work, which can make a real contribution towards reducing isolation. Vocational education affords the opportunity of in-depth study of work-related issues and can widen people's horizons by helping them understand their potential.

Whilst such training has been available for many other workers within Housing and Social Services departments for years, it is only relatively recently that it has become recognised as a need for wardens.

Although the Local Government Training Board (now the Local Government Management Board) proposed a programme of induction, basic and ongoing training for wardens as long ago as 1974, it was sadly not viewed as a priority by wardens' employers. Perhaps this was partly due to the fact that wardens employed in the 1950s, 1960s and 1970s were often paid on manual grades, regarded as on a par with caretakers and cleaners – frequently being expected to carry out some cleaning work themselves – and certainly rarely regarded as part of the organisational team. Not until the Institute of Housing initiated the National Wardens Certificated Course in 1986 was there any significant national recognition of the need for vocational education specifically designed round the needs of wardens. We are delighted to see how many wardens are enthusiastically participating in this course. An additional benefit has been the fact that many employers have begun to recognise and endorse the need for, and value of, all forms of training for their sheltered housing staff, and have increased their commitment to in-service training alongside sponsoring wardens on the National Wardens Certificated Course.

Re-defining the Role of the Warden

One result of the network of training opportunities now available across the country has been the opportunity it offers for large groups of wardens to discuss and evaluate their role. There appears to be a growing awareness of the need to re-define the role; we seem to have made the first step in recognising on a country-wide basis that the job is now significantly different from the traditional perception of the role. Wardens are taking it into their own hands to address the need for change, in the light of their recognition of themselves as professional workers, managing the care services which come into their schemes.

Changing the Job Title

Many wardens have expressed the view that the very title 'warden' is in itself a hindrance to a clear understanding of the remit of the job.

A number of wardens have told us of potential tenants who confuse it with the title 'warder' as in prison and who prior to living in sheltered housing imagine the warden to be, literally, a jailer, with a huge jangling bunch of keys. Similarly, wardens have said that when asked about their job at parties or other social occasions they have replied, rather vaguely 'I work with older people', feeling that this is preferable to facing the look of blank incomprehension which usually greets the sentence 'I'm a warden'. We have already seen how this lack of clarity about the warden's role leads to problems with regard to setting clear boundaries surrounding what wardens can and cannot be expected to do.

The Warden as a Scheme Manager

Changing the job title, then, would be more than a mere cosmetic exercise, it would be the beginning of a real re-definition of the role. Consensus on the new title to be used, however, may be difficult to reach. We favour the title 'Scheme Manager' as giving a clearer indication to the world at large about the purpose and scope of the job, although we are aware that some employers, particularly those whose attitudes towards the work of wardens are rooted in the past, are not happy about including any reference to management in the job title. Chapter 6 discusses the warden's role in the context of management and the need for the warden to recognise and use management skills when working with tenants. We hope that such initiatives as the National Certificated Course coupled with support from bodies such as the Institute of Housing and the National Wardens Association will keep this issue high on the agenda, ensuring plenty of opportunities for wardens to express and share their views, not only on the job title but on the future of the job itself.

Wardens as Professional Workers

Wardens, individually and collectively, must be the driving force behind the recognition of themselves as professionals, through their approach to the job. This initiative must be backed up and endorsed by wardens' employers who need to provide supportive and enlightened management policies in order to do so. Other groups who can support this are The National Wardens Association and the Institute of Housing (IOH). The IOH can be effective through its membership where wardens' issues can be kept high on the agenda at Branch Meetings, and through education programmes such as the National Certificated Wardens Course (NWCC) and the Advanced Certificated for wardens. Tutors of NWCC courses also have an important supportive role to play here. The National Wardens Association can provide a country-wide forum for discussion and debate, for it is wardens themselves who can and must be the main catalysts for change.

A combination of increased depth of knowledge and enhanced skills, leading to greater confidence and self esteem can enable wardens to begin the process of recognising themselves as professionals. In turn, this will affect the way in which other groups perceive them. For those wardens who have attended, or who are taking the year long National Certificated Wardens Course, group support and motivation for this task is easier to come by than for isolated and unsupported wardens who may frequently feel too overburdened with current responsibilities to have the energy to work for change. However, it is important to realise that your feelings are shared by others. We hope that reading aspects of this chapter, which distills the views and feelings that many wardens have expressed to us over the years, will contribute towards helping you feel less alone, and part of a network of like-minded colleagues.

Future Influences on the Role of the Warden

There are a number of further factors which seem likely to influence the way in which the role of the warden might develop in the future, amongst them the implications of the National Health and Community Care Act 1990. Once the Act is fully implemented in 1993, wardens should have a far greater input than ever before into the management of care for their residents; they should play an equal part in case conferences, and will be given opportunities to re-educate other professionals as to the scope and remit of their role. The content of the Act and its far reaching implications are discussed in Chapter 3. Some of the other issues which will affect the warden's role in the future concern current and proposed legislative changes regarding the provision of social housing. These are considered in Chapter 2.

Conclusion

We have seen how the role of the warden has developed, intrinsically linked with the somewhat *ad hoc* evolution of sheltered housing itself. We have looked at some of the major influences and pressures on wardens, who, through no fault of their own, have been the subject of unclear expectations, have had little support over the years, and who have, at times, appeared to be the victims of the effects of twenty years of somewhat unco-ordinated progress.

Given that further major changes in the care of the elderly and the role of the warden within the provision of such care are inevitable, it now seems time for wardens to take up the challenge of greeting the future positively. One of the most important ways in which wardens can take control is by re-defining their own role. For this to take place, there is a need for change in the attitude of wardens' own management, and that of other professionals towards the warden, yet this cannot happen until wardens themselves are clear about where the future lies.

For too long, the isolating and demoralising aspects of the job have tended towards discouraging wardens to think of themselves as anything other than 'only a warden'. But we have already seen that this is rapidly changing, and must continue to change for the 1990s and beyond – and it is wardens themselves who, through their own changed attitudes, can create the opportunities to establish their role as a profession in its own right.

References and Further Reading

Butler A (1989) 'The growth and development of alarm systems in sheltered housing' in M Fisk (ed) *Alarm Systems and Elderly People* Glasgow: The Planning Exchange.

Butler A, Oldman C and Greve J (1983) *Sheltered Housing for the Elderly: policy, practice and the consumer* London: George Allen & Unwin.

Clapham D and Munro M (1988) A comparison of Sheltered and Amenity housing for older people *Central Research Unit Paper* Scottish Office.

Clapham D and Munro M (1989) The role of sheltered housing wardens: conflict and change *Discussion paper no 21* University of Glasgow: Centre for Housing Research

Fisk M (1989) 'Right to Risk is paramount' in *Voluntary Housing* October 1989, pp. 16 & 17.
Fletcher P (1991) The future of sheltered housing – who cares? *Policy Report* National Federation of Housing Associations London/Anchor Housing Association.
1944 Ministry of Health *Housing Manual* 1944 London: HMSO.
Ministry of Housing and Local Government (1969) *Housing standards and costs: accommodation specially designed for old people* (circular 82/69) London.
Thompson, Lyn (1980) The role of central control in dispersed alarm systems in Butler A and Oldman C (eds) *Alarm Systems for the Elderly – report of a workshop* Department of Social Policy and Administration Research Monograph, University of Leeds.
Townsend, Peter (1962) *The Last Refuge* London: Routledge and Kegan Paul.

CHAPTER 2 Housing services and the warden

Introduction

Sheltered housing is one part of the range of social housing. This chapter considers the context of sheltered housing provision – local authorities, housing associations (including almshouses) and the private sector. The majority of wardens work within a housing framework. Although some wardens working for local authorities are managed by social services rather than by housing, generally the bricks and mortar are the responsibility of the housing authority, and the residents are tenants of the housing department. Housing association wardens need to have an understanding of the local authority from whom nominations to their scheme may come. Therefore, it is useful for wardens to have some idea of the background to, and wider policies of, housing organisations, so we begin this chapter by taking a brief look at the history and legislative framework surrounding public sector housing.

Next, we consider the need for wardens as members of a dispersed workforce to have an understanding of organisational structures. Being distant from head office, or from their area office, and not necessarily considered part of the team, decisions made at committee or chief officer level may take some time to filter down to wardens and may not be easily understood when they finally arrive. We have considered the need for wardens to be familiar with committee reports in Chapter 4. This is in order to be able to both write them yourself when necessary, and to understand those that you might receive regarding organisational policy and practice. In this way the organisation can begin to be demystified. We also encourage wardens to visit head office or the area office and make contacts with those who are just voices on the telephone – the repairs clerks, for example, or the allocations officer.

We look at what constitutes housing management and at how wardens can become more familiar with the housing management policies and practices which operate in their own employing organisations, and we examine the basic principles of housing finance that operate in local authorities and housing associations.

Since this book is being written at a time of enormous

proposed changes to the way social housing is provided and managed, we consider those changes and their possible effects on the warden service.

Finally, we examine the contribution made by the private sector to the provision of a range of housing options for older people.

Public Sector Housing : History and Legislative Framework

Local Authorities

A huge explosion in the demand for housing became apparent following the Industrial Revolution in the late-eighteenth and early-nineteenth centuries, when large numbers of people left the countryside and flocked to the towns and cities that were the sites of the factories providing them with employment. Houses were needed close to these factories and these were often built by speculative builders very quickly. Most had no sanitation or running water, and these unhygienic conditions often led to disease. The vast majority of such housing was privately owned, and frequently poorly managed – repairs left undone, whilst high rents were charged, often higher than those on low wages could afford, yet no alternative accommodation was available.

Octavia Hill pioneered housing management as we recognise it today. In 1865 she acquired the right to manage two tenanted houses in Marylebone, and her intention was to concern herself with the people who lived in the properties and their problems as well as taking responsibility for the property. She increased her portfolio of properties in management by persuading rich benefactors to invest in tenanted property which she managed by building up a relationship of trust with the tenants, offering them support when they got into difficulties, yet not taking over their lives, encouraging self help instead. As a result she rarely had a problem with rent arrears, and the management methods she adopted became a model of good practice which continues to have influence today.

There was, however, a clear need for a co-ordinated approach to the provision of housing for those who could not provide for themselves, and thus the state began to develop a role as housing provider.

From the late-nineteenth century onwards large numbers of Acts of Parliament were passed giving local authorities powers to build and manage properties. These began with the Housing of the

Working Classes Act in 1885, and many subsequent Acts were passed, widening the scope and powers of Local Authorities to provide housing and detailing the financial framework within which this could take place. Until 1949 all public sector housing was to be provided for the working classes but following the Housing Act 1949, Local Authorities were able to satisfy the requirements of all those perceived to be in housing need, regardless of class. By the 1970s, local authorities were not only providing a service to their existing tenants but with the introduction of the concept of the comprehensive housing service, to a wide range of others – homeless persons, grants for home improvements, the particular needs of those with disabilities etc. The 1977 Housing (Homeless Persons) Act gave local authorities a statutory duty to house people who were homeless, or threatened with homelessness if they had dependent children living with them, or if they were considered vulnerable due to old age, mental illness or handicap, physical disability or other special reason. (Following the 1977 Act, further legislation was passed in Part 3 (Homelessness) of the Housing Act 1985.)

The Housing Act 1980 gave secure tenants of council housing the right to buy their houses and to be granted a long lease on their flats. The 1980 Act also saw an extension of a number of further tenants rights, including those of information and consultation.

Much of the legislation within the 1980 Act, and other subsequent Housing Acts was consolidated within the 1985 Housing Act. A comprehensive description of housing legislation and its effects upon practice can be found in Mary Smith's *Guide to Housing* (1989) which is an invaluable book for all those wishing to deepen their historical understanding of the range of housing provision.

Housing Associations

In Chapter 1 the historical relationship between almshouses and sheltered housing was discussed. A strong ancestral relationship also exists between almshouses and the charitable housing associations with which we are familiar with today, since almshouses were probably the first type of housing provision built and managed by non-profit making bodies to meet the needs of people who were otherwise unable to organise accommodation for themselves. The voluntary housing sector, or housing association movement as it is known, continues that tradition today.

During the late-nineteenth and early-twentieth centuries, a number of wealthy philanthropists endowed trusts to provide housing for the working classes, including the Peabody Trust, the Guiness Trust, the Sutton Housing Trust and the Samuel Lewis Trust. These are organisations that we are familiar with today, coming under the umbrella of the voluntary housing movement, and providing general family housing, together with, as a later development, sheltered housing.

Following the first world war, a number of housing trusts and housing societies were formed to provide and manage family and general needs housing, largely in inner city areas, acting as a complement to the local authorities in whose areas they worked. Others met the needs of groups having specific needs – ex-servicemen for example, or women workers. The housing association movement continues the tradition of targeting groups with particular needs and responding by providing specially designed accommodation, in addition to providing family housing or general needs housing.

Following the 1948 National Assistance Act, financial subsidies were available for voluntary organisations to convert or build accommodation specifically for older people. Many existing and newly-formed housing associations began to consider the provision of what we now call sheltered housing from this point.

Two of the largest Housing Associations providing sheltered housing had their roots in the 1960s, and were set up by organisations having wider concern for the welfare of older people. The National Corporation for the Care of Old People – now the Centre for Policy on Ageing – enabled Hanover Housing Association to come into being in 1963. Hanover now has over 13,000 retirement properties. In 1968 the national charity Help the Aged set up the specialist housing association that we now know as Anchor Housing Association, and which is now a separate entity from its originating body.

The Housing Act 1964 set up the Housing Corporation to encourage the development of co-ownership housing societies. The Housing Corporation's role changed and developed over the years, as did the focus of the voluntary housing movement. By 1973 it was envisaged that a major expansion of the voluntary housing movement was a way to increase choice for those unable to afford to buy, and for whom the option of private rented accommodation was almost non-existent because of the decline of availability within this sector. Housing associations were seen as being a major force that would complement the range of accommodation provided through local authorities. Housing associations were encouraged not only to provide newly built housing stock but to refurbish and rehabilitate existing, usually privately owned, accommodation, thus playing a major role in regenerating decaying urban areas. The 1974 Housing Act encouraged a considerable expansion in the Housing Association movement. The Act was known as a charter for the movement, and strengthened the role of the government sponsored Housing Corporation – making it the main supervisory and financial agency through whom funding to the movement was channelled.

The 1980 Housing Act to which we have already referred also affected Housing Associations, particularly in the area of tenants' rights to information and consultation. Following considerable debate and pressure, in particular in the House of Lords, the right to buy was not given to tenants of charitable housing association properties.

The National Federation of Housing Associations is the independent umbrella body for Housing Associations, societies and trusts in England, concerned with disseminating information and ideas to its members, along with the provision of training. Additionally it represents the views of its members to central and local government and outside bodies. It also produces publications in the form of books and information leaflets, together with the monthly magazine *Voluntary Housing* and *Housing Associations Weekly*.

Up until the time of writing, the housing association movement has complemented and enhanced the work of local authorities in the provision of permanent rented accommodation for a variety of groups, including general needs housing and specialist accommodation, such as housing for the elderly and disabled, and the recovering mentally ill. However, current government initiatives are working towards the expansion of housing associations as the main providers and managers of social housing for the future, with local authorities playing a strategic role in assessing and planning housing needs rather than meeting them directly. Although in themselves, at local and national level, housing associations are independent of party political affiliation, it can be seen how the voluntary housing movement is subject to the differing policies of the party currently in government.

Organisational Structures

Understanding Structures

Few wardens working for local authorities seem to fully understand the structure and range of functions of the organisation for which they work. This is all the more regrettable when considering the fact that wardens are the front-line representatives of the employer, yet they may have little idea of how decisions are made, or by whom. We notice a similar phenomenon amongst some wardens working for housing associations, although where their employing organisation is small and locally based the warden often has greater contact with head office, and therefore a correspondingly greater understanding of policies, practices and personalities.

This is, of course, one of the factors associated with membership of a dispersed workforce. Generally those who work at head office, through a variety of formal and informal methods, sooner or later develop an understanding of organisational structure. Those with little or no opportunity for contact with the range of staff working at headquarters, their duties and responsibilities, or access to the written and spoken communication networks that operate within the organisation's offices often find it difficult to comprehend the scope of organisational activity. They may pick up bits of knowledge here and there, but without a concerted effort on their part and on that of their manager, their understanding of their own organisation may resemble a jigsaw puzzle with many of the key pieces missing.

We would encourage wardens to consider the general principles of organisational structures within housing departments and housing associations through which they can deepen their understanding of their own employing organisation in particular. One way to do this is to consider a structure or hierarchy chart pertaining to your employing organisation. The chart will give a diagrammatic picture of the way responsibility is devolved outwards and downwards through your organisation, and can enable you to see who is responsible for what, and how all the different sections and departments interact and support one another to provide services for the ultimate consumer, the tenant. It can also help you to see which sections of the organisation you know little about; if this is the case, we would encourage you to find out more about them in order to complete your own organisational jigsaw. In the six years of carrying out this process on the National Wardens Certificated Course at the College of North East London we have noticed a significant change in the way wardens are presented on structure charts. In the early days, they frequently did not feature at all – the chart ended with their managers. Nowadays, however, evidence of the greater significance that is being afforded to sheltered housing is shown by in the fact that most wardens now feature prominently on structure charts – though sadly not yet on all those that we see. There is often a link, in larger organisations especially, between specific management support for wardens and an increased organisational awareness of their importance. This is examined in Chapter 7, in the section entitled 'Wardens and their Managers'.

Some basic information about the way in which local authority housing departments and housing associations are structured and managed in terms of the responsibilities of elected members/committee members and the way in which officers carry out the policies set by members follows, which should complement the brief history and statutory framework outlined earlier in this chapter.

Committee Structures

Local Authorities

Policies and practices with regard to local authority housing are determined by the members of the Housing Committee (or similar title) who are politicians, locally elected councillors. Needless to say, housing policy at a local level reflects the overall housing strategies of the nationally elected government of the day but is of course greatly influenced by other factors such as the political party in power at local level plus the housing needs and stresses of the particular area in question.

The Chief Officer of the Housing Department – often called the Director of Housing – has the task of ensuring that decisions made by the Housing Committee are carried out. Whilst the Director often has a high degree of autonomy in terms of how policies determined at committee level are put into practice, the formulation of policies and strategies are the responsibility of the elected members. In practice this happens through a process of reports to committee, usually prepared by officers, with proposals or recommendations for action. Members debate the ideas and proposals contained within these reports and endorse or amend the action proposed. It is then the responsibility of the Director to ensure this action is carried out. Officers therefore have an advisory responsibility towards the elected members, (rather as civil servants have towards government ministers) together with executive responsibility to ensure policy implementation. It is because reports to committee, together with internal reports which disseminate information regarding policies and practices, are such a vital element of the communication structure of any organisation that we encourage wardens to fully develop their skills in report reading and writing (see Chapter 4).

Responsibility within the housing organisation is devolved downwards from the Director through a series of management tiers. Responsibility for the various services provided – allocations, homelessness and advice, housing management, housing repairs and maintenance, development, the private sector are some examples of how departments can be divided up – is given to Assistant Directors or Principal Officers, who have a team (or teams) of officers reporting to them.

Housing Associations
All charitable housing associations are controlled by a committee of management, elected by the members of the association. Such members are not paid, giving their time and expertise to the association on a purely voluntary basis. Neither does the organisation operate on a profit-making basis, hence the name 'Voluntary Housing Movement'. Many housing associations have strong tenant representation on their committees. The committee structure may be divided into a series of sub-committees, which may be regional in nature, for example, in the case of a housing association having properties in various areas, or which may be formed to consider particular aspects of policy, such as finance, development, housing management etc. In all cases, regional or sub-committees report to the main committee, or board, which is responsible for every aspect of the housing association's day-to-day activities.

Authority is delegated to staff by the committee through the association's chief officer, similar to the local authority committee model. Similarly, responsibility for activities within the organisation is developed downwards through a series of tiers of officers, although there is a far greater variety of sizes of organisation represented within the Housing Association movement. Some are very small indeed, having perhaps only two or three paid staff, whilst others, as we have seen, may own many properties and therefore have a correspondingly large management structure. It should be emphasised that, as with local authorities, the staff carry out the policies and practices determined by the committee members to whom they report.

Housing Management

An understanding of the basic principles of housing management is helpful for wardens. Although some wardens working in the public sector are employed by social services departments, the properties in which they work are usually managed by the local housing authority of which their residents are tenants. The section with whom they will probably have the most contact will be housing management. Wardens working within local authority housing departments, and their counterparts in housing associations will usually be part of the housing management team. Private sector wardens will, in most cases, be employed by an organisation whose purpose is to manage the properties. Although housing management, including responsibility for repairs and maintenance, is only one aspect of the overall provision of housing, it is a vital area, linking as it does the good housekeeping elements of maintaining the bricks and mortar in good repair with the support of the tenants of the properties, rather as Octavia Hill set out to do in the nineteenth century.

In order for wardens to feel confident in representing their organisation through their day-to-day contact with tenants and their relatives, together with other professionals, it is important to have a clear understanding of the work carried out by the housing management team. A good way to start this process is to spend some time with an **estate officer** or **housing officer**. The job title will vary in different organisations but the purpose of the post will be to have responsibility for managing a number of properties. Depending on the organisation, this number can vary between 150 and 1000; whatever the figure, the officer will be the tenants' first point of contact with the organisation. Responsibilities too will vary, but are likely to include dealing with rent arrears, monitoring repairs, debt counselling, neighbour disputes, applications for transfer, and contraventions of tenancy conditions, all in respect of individual tenants, together with liaising with groups of tenants, supporting tenants associations and encouraging tenant participation.

As we saw in Chapter 1, housing officers may also have responsibility for managing estate-based staff, such as wardens and caretakers, where these services are not managed by a separate section.

Wardens can also benefit from spending time in the **repairs section**, looking at how procedures work, and getting some experience of policies and practices designed to keep properties in good repair, such as routine and cyclical maintenance programmes, and how emergency repairs are dealt with. An additional benefit of this exercise for wardens as members of a dispersed workforce, with little contact with the central point, is to put faces to names when spending time at head office – helpful for future telephone contact when reporting or chasing repairs.

A further aspect of managing housing with direct application and relevance to the work of wardens is the way properties are allocated and let to tenants. We encourage wardens to familiarise themselves with the **allocations policies and procedures** of their own organisations, whether local authorities or housing associations. Housing association wardens can also benefit from an understanding of the selection and allocations procedures operating both in their own organisations and in the local authority in which their scheme is located, since in many cases, nominations to their scheme will come from the local authority. Wardens often complain of inappropriate allocations to their schemes; setting up a good two-way communication process between themselves and those responsible for making allocations to sheltered housing, including providing up-to-date information on current levels of frailty on their schemes, and perhaps inviting allocations officers to visit from time to time, can often help this situation. Spending some time with allocations officers also helps wardens to understand some of the wider responsibilities of the organisation such as dealing with homelessness, and the various priority groups whose needs must be taken into account when making allocations, and enables a recognition of the pressures involved in this aspect of social housing.

Wardens working in the private sector have a different perspective on this aspect of managing housing, since in general their residents choose to buy into their schemes. Generally only those within a certain age group can live there – often they have to be over 55 years of age, for example, although younger relatives could buy a flat on behalf of their parents. Many private sector wardens are themselves involved in the sale of flats on their schemes. However, the tenancy and repairs and maintenance aspects of managing private sector schemes will have parallels with those in the public sector, and we would encourage private sector wardens to familiarise themselves with the way these are carried out in their own organisations.

Some of the wider aspects of managing housing include the way in which **rents** are collected, the way in which overall **finances** are administered, including rent-setting policies and capital expenditure on the housing stock, and the consideration of overall **policy issues**, including legislative changes and their effects. We would encourage wardens to develop an understanding of how these areas are tackled within their organisations.

As we have seen, over the past ten or twelve years, there have been moves towards increasing accountability to tenants of social housing, and one way in which this has been achieved, particularly by local authorities, is by decentralising. Instead of all the management functions taking place at one head office, local area offices have opened up, having delegated authority to carry out most or all aspects of the housing management function for a specific geographical area. Further changes that will affect the way that social housing is managed are considered later in this chapter.

Housing Finance

An understanding of the basic principles that lie behind the financial aspects of public sector housing can help wardens understand the wider aspects of their employing organisations, and in particular the pressures under which they operate. What follows is a very basic outline of the principles; those wanting to know more are referred to Aughton and Malpass (1990) to provide more information on this subject and to gain explanations of some of the jargon and unfamiliar concepts.

Possibly the most basic concept to master is the difference between capital expenditure and revenue expenditure.

Revenue expenditure or running costs, consists of recurring annual expenditure such as salaries, loan interest, day-to-day maintenance and office costs.

Capital expenditure comprises the one-off purchases or investments – the permanent assets of the organisation, such as buildings, vehicles etc.

Most of the expenditure incurred by organisations running a housing service falls into these two categories, although some aspects of repairing properties fall in the middle. If the repair enhances the value of the property, such as providing a new roof then it counts as capital expenditure. If it is simply keeping the property going – fixing a dripping tap or a leaky radiator for example – then it is revenue expenditure.

Capital Expenditure

Capital available within **local authorities** takes the form of a loan taken out by the council to invest in building or repairing properties or purchasing land or equipment, and which is paid back over long periods. In the case of money raised to build houses, the repayment period is generally 60 years – the average life of a house. The amount of money each local authority can spend on building or repairing housing each year is determined by the Housing Investment Programme (HIP), in which local authorities bid for funding every September. These bids are based on the authorities' assessment of housing need and the money necessary to meet this in the coming year. The Department of the Environment (DoE) decides how much each authority will be able to spend on capital projects on the basis of the authority's bid together with the DoE's judgement as to how well the authority manages its existing properties. This announcement is normally made in the January following the bid.

Housing associations operate under a different system, which has changed significantly since 1989. Before this date, the government, through the Housing Corporation, would give Housing Association Grants (HAG) to cover the capital cost of any new project, such as a new build scheme or major refurbishment or repairs. The amount given was calculated on the basis of how far the rental income was likely to meet the costs of the project, and then HAG would make up the difference. Rents were fixed by the rent officer, and the HAG grant, in making up the shortfall, would be given up to a limit determined by the Housing Corporation.

Whilst special needs schemes still qualify for full HAG, the situation for other types of housing association projects which need capital funding has significantly changed since 1989.

Instead of the HAG being flexible and the rents fixed, it now works the other way round; HAG forms a considerably smaller proportion of the cost of new build housing. Associations are encouraged to seek loans in the private sector and to charge higher rents than before to make up the shortfall. Housing associations themselves set the rents instead of the rent officer.

Revenue Expenditure

Within **local authority** housing departments, the Housing Revenue Account (HRA) shows the revenue expenditure transactions which take place. This is shown in Figure 2.1.

We can see that what goes into the account is:

- housing subsidy, from central government;
- income from rents;
- income from service charges;
- income from interest on capital receipts (sale of council houses);

and that this must pay for:

- loan interest;
- management costs (including staff costs);
- maintenance costs;
- housing benefits.

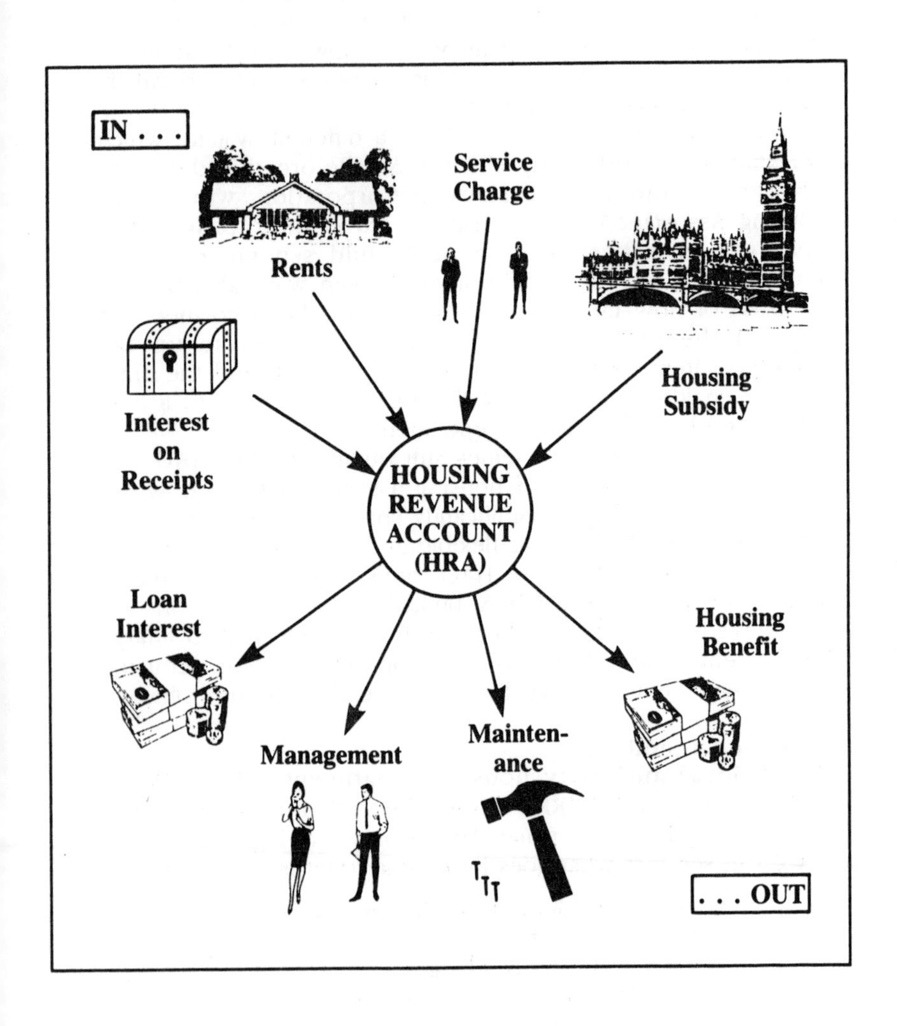
IN . . .
Service
Charge
Rents
Housing
Subsidy
Interest
on
Receipts
HOUSING
REVENUE
ACCOUNT
(HRA)
Loan
Interest
Housing
Benefit
Mainten-
ance
Management
. . . OUT

Fig 2.1

Not only must the account balance, but it is also 'ring-fenced,' meaning that none of the costs can be met from other sources, such as general funds – poll tax money. In other words, the housing department does not have access to the authority's wider funds in order to meet any of these revenue costs. This is a particular issue for wardens at the moment, as there is a question mark over whether the warden service can continue to be paid for through the HRA, following a court case known as 'the Ealing Judgment' (DoE 1992). This is discussed later in this chapter, in the section entitled 'Future funding of the local authority warden service'.

Housing associations are facing a different set of problems with regard to revenue expenditure. As we have seen, there is now an obligation for housing associations to borrow in the private sector and, in many cases, to charge rents which will cover costs. However, there is also an obligation for housing associations to keep rents 'affordable', although this term has never been defined by the government. The National Federation of Housing Associations has, as an indicative guide, suggested that housing costs should be not more than 22 per cent of tenants' average income, but many associations are finding that rent levels have to be considerably higher than this in order for costs to be met. In some cases housing benefit does not cover the full rent because the rent is too high.

In special needs schemes, including sheltered housing, capital finance is through HAG, together with special needs management allowances (SNMA) to cover the increased costs of providing such housing. However, in schemes where care is provided, such as extra-care sheltered schemes, this is not covered by housing benefit. Many of the elderly tenants will be on low fixed incomes, and may need income support to cover the costs of the care they need.

In housing association sheltered schemes, the cost of the warden service is met through a service charge paid by each tenant. This is separate from the rent, which pays for the property itself. The service charge also pays for the upkeep of the communal areas of the schemes, including common rooms, heated corridors etc. Because housing association tenants are entitled to receive a detailed explanation of how the money they pay each week is spent, they can easily identify how much they pay towards the warden's salary, accommodation, and in some cases items such as the warden's phone bill. Whilst it is important for tenants to be able to see how their money is used, it does of course mean that information about the warden becomes common property, and contributes further to the lack of privacy experienced by the warden, which we first considered in Chapter 1.

Future funding of the Local Authority Warden Service

Until now the services provided by local authority wardens have been funded through the HRA. However, there is now a question over how local authority wardens will be funded in the future, following a court case known as 'The Ealing Judgment'.

The Ealing Judgment concerns a tenant of the London Borough of Ealing who argued that 'care' services provided by the warden of sheltered housing should not have to be paid for through the HRA. This view was upheld by the Court of Appeal and the tenant won the case.

Because decisions made by Courts of Appeal, together with the reasons for the judgments, form the basis of case law and set precedents for other cases, it has been necessary to consider the repercussions of the Ealing Judgment for all local authorities providing warden services.

Therefore the Department of the Environment (DoE), as the government department responsible for local authority housing, prepared and circulated a consultation paper in response to the judgment, proposing an interim strategy to give local authorities temporary powers to continue current funding arrangements pending a final decision on how, and by whom, the 'care' elements of the warden service should be funded from April 1994.

By restricting itself to the financial implications of the case the DoE paper ignored the wider implications raised by the judgment. The paper failed to define 'care' in the context of the judgment, thus leaving open to question whether tasks carried out by others working in social housing could also come under this heading. This, in turn, would mean that they too would fail to qualify for funding through the HRA.

Further, the paper is based on an untypical and unrepresentative picture of the role of the warden. Some of the examples it gives of tasks carried out by the warden include toiletting, bathing, shaving, dressing and feeding tenants, together with giving medication and nursing care. It is hard to dispute the fact that such tasks should not be paid for out of the HRA; they are social and medical services, and should be both provided and funded by the appropriate authority. What is in dispute is the extent to which wardens carry out these tasks on anything other than an emergency basis, if at all. It appears that the role of the warden has been confused with that of a carer in a Part 3 home, and shows a worrying lack of awareness on the part of the DoE. At the time of writing, this issue is still at the consultation stage. Whilst there is talk of transferring the costs of the local authority warden service to the social services budget, it is premature to assume that this will be the case. Responses to the DoE from a number of those consulted, including the Institute of Housing, have pointed out the need to consider the wider implications of the judgment, to define 'care' and to provide a more accurate definition of the role of the warden, before legislation is enacted.

Current Issues and Future Possibilities

The Customer focus

Over the past ten years or so there has been an increasing perception of the tenant of public sector housing as a customer, rather than as a grateful recipient of services provided. The emphasis on information and consultation which we saw in the 1980 Housing Act has been further consolidated in subsequent legislation, and both local authorities and housing associations have an obligation to ensure tenant participation, resulting in an improvement in the landlord/tenant relationship, an increase in tenant – or customer – satisfaction with the service provision and ultimately an improvement in conditions, particularly on the larger and more run-down council estates. Anne Power (1987) documents the considerable contribution to the improvement of run-down estates made by the Priority Estates Project, which placed emphasis upon the involvement of tenants at every stage of the improvement and rehabilitation process.

This increased emphasis on customer satisfaction has led to a change in climate and attitude within public sector housing. Issues are considered increasingly from the perspective of the tenant, or consumer of the service, and tenant participation continues to be an important organisational strategy.

Quality

In tandem with the customer-orientated approach goes an emphasis on the quality of the service provided. Increasingly, public sector housing organisations are measuring the consistency of their provision and the value for money their customers receive. Clearly-defined targets are identified in terms of levels of service and responses to customer queries and requests. In other words, customers should know what to expect when they call on a service provided by a housing organisation, whether this be the repairs service, for example, or the central control alarm. Clearly-defined response times are one important measurable aspect of service which everyone understands. Performances in every area are monitored and evaluated, and customer feedback is taken seriously. One important aspect of quality control within an organisation is that the staff at every level should be involved with service evaluation and target setting. As an example of how this may influence the sheltered housing service, at the time of writing, LB Hillingdon is currently applying for the British Quality Standard BS 5750 to cover its alarm control centre, largely on the basis of consistency of approach – so its customers know exactly what they can expect when they call on this service. A number of local authorities and housing and housing associations have already successfully implemented quality strategies throughout their organisations. Two examples are documented by the Institute of Housing (Catterick 1992) together with an in-depth consideration of the implementation of quality strategies within social housing.

Compulsory Competitive Tendering (CCT)

At the time of writing, housing organisations are debating the government's consultation paper on the compulsory competitive tendering of housing management services. In practice, this means that instead of automatically managing their housing stock, local authority departments will tender for the job, along with any other organisation which considers it might be able to do so – such as a housing association or an estate agent with a property management portfolio, for example. Clearly, to win the tender to manage the property, housing departments are having to ensure that their performance is both cost effective and streamlined. Outdated and cumbersome bureaucratic procedures have no place in such an environment, and therefore organisations are having to manage staff and finances on commercial, business-orientated lines.

This initiative is a further element of the government's strategy for local authorities to move away from being direct providers of services. They will remain accountable for the quality of service provision through monitoring, and they will retain some strategic policy responsibilities, including planning how homelessness is coped with, overall allocations policies, financial planning and repairs programmes. Local authorities will have to produce an annual report for all tenants covering every aspect of housing provision and performance.

It is difficult to predict the effects of this on sheltered housing; however, the housing management responsibilities of the sheltered housing warden are specifically mentioned within the DoEs consultation paper on the subject (DoE/Welsh Office 1992) as being one element of the housing management function that should be considered when drawing up a tender specification. Given that the warden's role is not clearly defined at present, the examination of the role, and resulting clarification may be of benefit, particularly where wardens themselves are fully involved in the exercise.

Voluntary Transfer of housing stock

The 1986 Housing and Planning Act and the 1988 Housing Act opened the way for local authorities to transfer their housing stock and management responsibilities to other landlords. This, together with compulsory competitive tendering, is part of the Government's strategy for local authorities to move towards becoming enablers rather than direct providers of housing. Although it was originally envisaged that existing charitable housing associations would be appropriate new landlords, few have, in fact, become so. However, some authorities have nevertheless transferred their stock to housing associations that they themselves have set up. Transfer has to follow consultation with tenants, a majority of whom must vote in favour of such action. Local authorities set up a provisional housing association committee structure, consult with tenants, and, if the vote is in favour of the transfer, the new housing association is ready to manage the properties. Where such large scale voluntary transfers have taken place, many, if not all, of the former officers of the council housing department have moved over to become the staff of the housing association following final government approval for the transfer. Generally, the argument which has swayed tenants to vote for the transfer of their properties to the newly formed housing association is the prospect that rents may be kept at lower levels, since greater financial subsidies are available to housing associations than to local authorities. However, by no means all those local authorities who have chosen the transfer route have received a 'yes' vote from their tenants, perhaps showing that there is less dissatisfaction with the local authority as landlord than was originally estimated. As we have seen, there is a strong likelihood that compulsory competitive tendering (CCT) of the local authority housing management function will see properties being managed by, amongst others, housing associations should housing departments themselves not win the tenders. However, CCT will not be required from former local authority housing transferred through voluntary transfer.

Private Sector Initiatives for Older People

Private Sheltered Housing

This type of housebuilding largely took off in the 1980s when developers became aware of the increasing numbers of owner occupiers whose families had left home and who therefore wished to move into smaller, purpose built accommodation, having a warden on site and perhaps also with some communal facilities available. Much of this type of accommodation is built by private developers, and flats or bungalows in such developments are offered on long leases for outright sale on the open market. Purchasers normally buy a 99-year lease on such properties, and enter into an agreement regarding the services and management charges. Although anyone can buy a lease on such properties, they can normally only be occupied by those over 55 years of age.

Residents in such schemes pay a service charge covering the costs of the resident warden (who is sometimes called housekeeper or house manager), caretaking, cleaning and other communal services. One disadvantage for older people living on a fixed income and having used all their capital to buy into the scheme is that service charges may rise to keep pace with inflation, unlike their pensions, and it may be hard to manage financially as a result.

Housing associations have an increasingly important role to play with regard to these schemes; their specifically set up non-charitable arms are often to be found managing such schemes, initially built by private developers. Both Hanover and Anchor (through its Guardian subsidiary) are involved in this way. Other privately built schemes are managed by companies set up for this purpose – Peverals, a subsidiary of McCarthy and Stone, one of the largest builders of retirement schemes, and Retirement Care, a private company set up specifically to manage leasehold sheltered housing, are two examples.

Although there is no regulatory body controlling such housing a national working party was set up in 1983 by the National Housing and Town Planning Council (NHTPC) and the House Builders Federation to draw up guidelines for those building and managing such housing. Additionally, Age Concern England and the NHTPC have produced a buyer's guide to sheltered housing designed to ensure potential purchasers find out as much as possible about what is available prior to purchase.

Leasehold Schemes for the Elderly (LSE) were developed by the housing association movement in recognition that some older people did not have sufficient capital to buy sheltered housing outright, but could make a substantial contribution towards the cost. A proportion of the cost of the lease was contributed by the purchaser therefore, with the housing association making up the rest through HAG. Housing associations retained the freehold of the building, and managed the properties, with the leaseholders paying a service charge to cover this.

Sales of private sheltered homes have been affected by the recession in the general housing market since 1989. It is likely that the demand is still there, but the existing property belonging to those wishing to move in is not selling in the current housing market.

This is an interesting area for public sector wardens to consider; feedback from our students who visit such schemes indicates that private sector wardens, especially those who are not employed by the housing association management organisations, are operating under vastly different terms and conditions of service to public sector wardens, with contrasting expectations of the warden's role from the residents of the schemes. Mobile wardens operating from local authority alarm control centres may also provide emergency cover to such tenants in the absence of their own warden and it is helpful for them to have an understanding of the differences between their own organisation and those operating in the private sector.

'Staying Put'

There are a variety of ways in which elderly owner occupiers, unable to cope practically or financially with home ownership, yet who do not wish to leave their familiar surroundings, may remain in their own homes. Schemes such as Anchor Housing Association's *Staying Put* initiative provide, through agency services, practical help, advice and support. It must be remembered that however bad their housing conditions, many older people find the prospect of having the necessary improvements carried out quite daunting, as documented by Rose Wheeler (1985). Organisations and initiatives such as *Staying Put* and *Care and Repair Ltd*, sponsored by Shelter amongst others, can provide the necessary sympathetic assistance and support. A selection of publications giving further information on this subject can be found in the reading list at the end of this chapter.

A valuable service which can help vulnerable older people stay in their own homes is the provision of dispersed alarm units, linked to local authority centres. This is another area which may particularly interest mobile wardens since they may well be answering alarm calls from older people living in their own homes in the community.

References and Further Reading

Age Concern/National Housing and Town Planning Group *A Buyers guide to sheltered housing: a guide for potential purchasers, their families and advisers* (3rd edition 1989) London: Age Concern.

Aughton, Henry with Malpass, Peter (1990) *Housing Finance – a basic guide* London: Shelter.

Catterick, Peter (1992) *Total quality: an introduction to quality management in social housing* Coventry Institute of Housing.

Cope, Helen (1990) *Housing Associations: Policy and Practice* Macmillan.

Department of the Environment/Welsh Office Consultation Paper (June 1992) *Competing for Quality in Housing: competition in the provision of Housing Management.*

Department of the Environment Consulation paper (September 1992) *Local government & housing act 1989: Warden services in the Housing Revenue Account: Consequences of the Ealing judgment.*

National Consumer Council (1991) *Informing your tenants – a guide for local housing authorities*, London: National Consumer Council.

National Federation of Housing Associations *Committee Members Handbook* (1984, reprinted 1985) London: NFHA.

Power, Anne (1987) *Property before people: the Management of twentieth century council housing* London: Allen and Unwin.

Smith, Mary E H (1971) *Guide to Housing* (3rd edition 1989) London: Housing Centre Trust.

Wheeler, Rose 1985 *Don't move, we've got you covered: a study of the Anchor Housing Trust Staying Put Scheme* London: Institute of Housing.

CHAPTER 3 Social Services and Older People

Introduction

Statutory, private and voluntary provision of care for older people has developed in a piecemeal fashion. New wardens discover that a variety of departments and organisations provide services and that these are often confusing, unco-ordinated and difficult to obtain. In this chapter we propose to unravel and explain these services and problems using two complementary approaches, as well as outline the details of the Community Care changes. Note that we have focused on **services** for older people and refer readers wishing to learn about money benefits to the excellent Sally West, Age Concern publication listed in the references at the end of this chapter.

Our first approach compartmentalises the care a person receives according to where it is given, and the second divides the care according to who provides it.

Hence we shall firstly look at community, residential, home and day care, and secondly explore statutory, private, voluntary and family care.

We conclude with some observations on the rationing of services to users. But first we will begin with the context in which so many changes are taking place.

An Ageing Population

Almost every adult in the country knows that there have been important demographic changes regarding older people. Put simply, we have seen an increase in the actual number of older people in Great Britain and an increase in the proportion of them compared to all those under retirement age. In particular there has been, and will continue to be a significant growth in the number of very elderly people – significant because the over 75s are more likely to need social and health care than younger elderly people.

Increase in number of Older People

Figure 3.1 shows the increase in the actual number of elderly people this century and projected trends into the next. The

Fig 3.1 The elderly population: past, present and future Great Britain

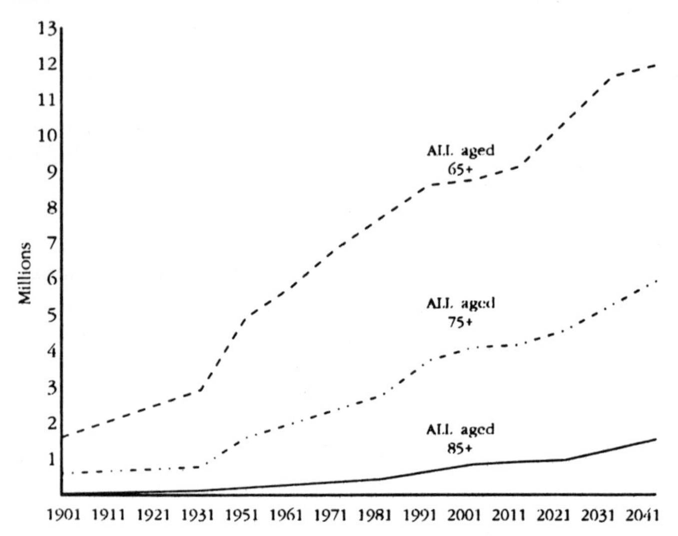

Source: Family Policy Studies Centre Fact Sheet 2 1991

increase in the number of older people in the population is the result of increased life expectancy which is now an average of 72 for men and 78 for women. Men and women born between 1910–12 could expect to live only an average of 53 years. Hence the people in your schemes are the survivors, the exceptions.

Figure 3.1 shows the significant increase in the number of over 75s between 1981 and 2001, i.e. 3,053,000 to 4,309,000, i.e. 1.3 million more very elderly people. This represents a growth from 44 per cent to 47 per cent of the elderly population. By 2001 there will be over one million people aged 85 and over, representing 13 per cent of all elderly people.

Increase in Proportion of Older People

Figure 3.2 shows how there has been a remarkable increase in the proportion of the population aged over 65 since the beginning of the century.

Fig 3.2 Percentage of the population aged 65+ 1901–2041 Great Britain

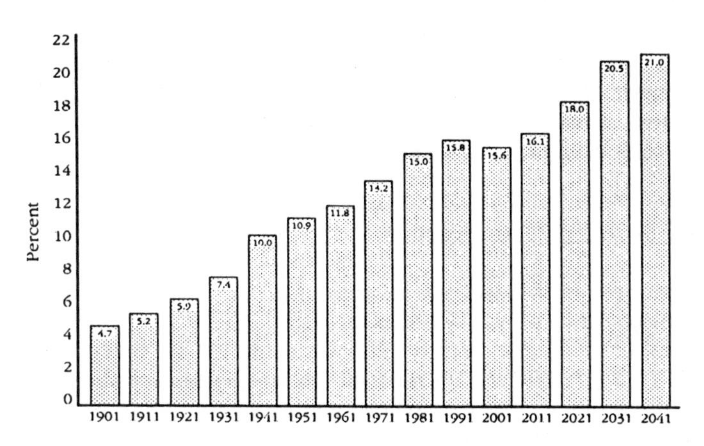

Source: Family Policy Studies Centre Fact Sheet 2 1991

The apparent steadying of the percentage (15 per cent–15.6 per cent) of older people between 1981 and 2001 is deceptive as this conceals the slight decline in numbers of young elderly and the rise of old elderly that was apparent in figure 3.1.

Ethnic Minority Elderly

There are regional variations in the proportion of older people in the population. We encourage wardens to find out from their library or local authority the pattern of age distribution in their own area and to make special enquiries about the age profile of the range of ethnic minority groups. Currently, only 4.5 per cent of ethnic minorities nationally are over 60 but as the ethnic population ages the percentage will become more similar to that of the white population.

There are differences between ethnic minority groups which reflect patterns of immigration over the last 40 years. There will be a rapid increase in the number of elderly people of West Indian origin between 1992 and 2011. The main increase in the number of older people in the Indian, Pakistan, Bangladeshi communities will come after 2021. Ethnic minority communities are currently concentrated in metropolitan areas and Greater London and wardens from these areas often acquire considerable expertise and local knowledge about ethnic elderly people, their needs and specialist services available.

Women

There are significantly more older women than men so the proportion of women in the population increases with age. In 1991 60 per cent of the population aged 65 or over were women. This proportion rose to 85 per cent in the 85+ age group. Between two-thirds and three-quarters of sheltered housing residents are women.

Household Composition

Changes in household composition is another significant demographic trend. There is projected to be an increase in the number of single-person older households between 1991 and 2001 of 335,000 to 3.3 million. Three-quarters of these will be single women, many of whom will be living alone as a result of the death of their spouse.

Disability

Most older people live independently but there is an increased likelihood of disability and therefore dependency of some kind with advancing age. Figure 3.3 below shows how:

Fig 3.3 The prevalence of disability among the population in Great Britain by age

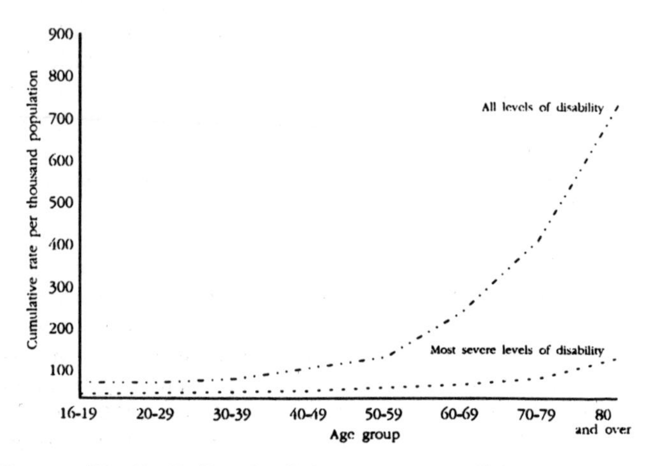

Source: Family Policy Studies Centre Fact Sheet 2 1992

> disability rates start to climb steadily after 50 becoming particularly steep over 70. The most severe levels of disability remain low until about 70 and then rise quickly. From about 75 more people have some level of disability than do not. Increasing disability with age means a growing dependency on others. Nearly one half of those 85+ are unable to walk down the road unaided and nearly a third cannot manage stairs unaided.
>
> (Family Policy Studies Centre 1991)

Divorce

The rise in the divorce rate has implications for social policy and older people. Currently very few people enter old age as divorcees – in 1990 one in 39 women aged 65+ and one in 44 men were divorced. By 2025 these proportions are expected to be one in 8 and one in 12.

So far we have tried to heighten awareness of recent and projected demographic changes relating to older people. We would now like to balance the apparently negative connotations of these changes with a more positive perspective on the health and activities of older people.

Contribution of Older People

It is commonly implied that all people over retirement age are somehow a burden on society. We ignore the enormous contribution that many older people, especially the newly retired or young elderly, make to society in the form of caring for others or as volunteers. Fifty-nine per cent of elderly carers spend 50 hours or more per week caring. This care is usually given by a husband or wife and underlies the significance of the spouse as the first source of care in old age, and the implications of the rising divorce figures commented on above. One study found that 43 per cent of the over 65s help other older people (Thane 1987).

Disability Over-emphasised

The statistics on the association between disability and increasing age can be over-emphasised. Not all very elderly people become frail or dependent. For example 80 per cent of the over 80s have no dementia, 90 per cent of the over 75s are not housebound. Old age is not an illness, despite the ageist assumptions to the contrary that we explore in Chapter 5. Much ill health in older people is preventable and/or treatable yet all too often attitudes such as 'what do you expect at their/my age' lead to lack of diagnosis or treatment.

Community Care

In this section we will look at the background to community care policies, at the problems of implementing them and at the details and effects of the solutions to some of these problems as put forward by Sir Roy Griffiths and the government in the White Paper *'Caring for Older People: Community Care into the Next Decade and Beyond'* (Cmmd 849 1989) and the NHS and Community Care Act 1990. We will conclude by summarising our views on how wardens can make an impact on the changes currently taking place.

Background

There are many reasons why community care has been a popular policy for several decades. It could be said to have begun in the 1940s – research showed that children were damaged by being removed from their mothers and suffered from the regimentation and loss of individuality in children's homes. During the 1950s a belief in community care developed in regard to another client group – the mentally ill – due to widespread optimism about newly developed drugs to treat the symptoms of mental illness. In the early 1960s the Minister of Health, Enoch Powell, announced that all mental hospitals would be closed and patients decanted either to the community or to psychiatric wards of district general hospitals. The 'anti-institutional' care movement gained momentum with extensive media coverage of scandalous treatment in mental illness and mental handicap hospitals in the 1960s and 1970s. The work of academic sociologists such as Irving Goffman highlighted the harmful effects of institutional care and the concept of institutionalisation was introduced to the public and professionals alike.

During the 1970s successive governments continued to promote community care policy in preference to residential care, partly because the former was considered to be cheaper (and reducing public expenditure became a political imperative after the oil crisis in 1973) and partly because of an awareness of the implications of an ageing population in the last quarter of this century (see preceding section). New technology (such as alarms, aids etc.) also helped enable people to live in their own or in specially built homes for independent living.

The final influence on community care has been 'normalisation' philosophy which stems from the civil rights movement in the USA in the 1960s. We refer to this in Chapter 5 where we discuss the rights of elderly people to lead as near normal a life as possible accepting, if necessary, some degree of risk.

Problems of Community Care in the 1970s and 1980s

Yet despite all these imperatives towards community care, the policy was not a success. The Audit Commission produced a report in 1986 documenting the many problems of community care which, put simply, amounted to poor co-ordination and organisation, and illogical funding. Outside the Audit Commission's remit to comment on were problems of inadequate resources and NIMBY ('Not In My Back Yard') attitudes towards various client groups.

Inadequate resources – since 1975 successive governments have tried to hold back public expenditure. Most statutory community care comes from local authority social services departments (SSDs) and the NHS. Local authorities have increasingly to control their expenditure to avoid government penalties and the NHS is also cash-limited. Professionals and managers within these services continue to complain that they are asked to provide services but not given the resources to do so.

Illogical funding – the Audit Commission referred to the 'perverse incentive' of the social security system towards funding private residential care but not its community care alternatives. The Audit Commission also commented on the limitations of the dowry and bridging systems related to the transfer of patients from NHS to local authority care.

Poor organisation – or 'organisational fragmentation and confusion'. The main statutory organisations providing community care services, the NHS and SSDs, are quite different in their functions, objectives, structures, accountability, funding, culture and priorities. In the early 1940s the civil service of the coalition war government proposed that the new NHS should come under local government control but this was rejected by doctors. With hindsight it is easy to observe how much easier it would be to implement community care now, had the doctors not taken this line. Not only easier to implement for the professionals, including wardens, but more comprehensive and seamless for the customers or users of services. For the client cares little who is providing the service or the professional niceties of job descriptions or for the buck-passing between health, social and housing departments. The fragmented and confusing organisation of care contributes to omissions, narrow assessments and delays.

The NHS and the Social Services reorganised in the 1970s. Again with hindsight it is tempting to regret and scorn the attempt, in these reorganisations, to rigidly divide health and social needs and to place all health care professionals under the NHS and all social care professionals in the new Social Services Departments of the local authority.

NIMBY – i.e. community care is a good idea unless it disturbs people or property prices. Most of us have fears and prejudices, and wardens often have to deal with the resentments and misunderstandings of neighbours or other residents in a scheme, if a tenant is mentally ill or has unconventional habits, or exhibits challenging behaviour.

The Audit Commission report confirmed the worst fears about the way the policy of successive governments was failing elderly, mentally ill, mentally handicapped and disabled people. Progress towards community care was very slow for all client groups especially the mentally ill.

Suggested Solutions

The Audit Commission outlined a number of options to remedy these deficiencies but recommended that a high level enquiry be set up to explore these options more fully. The possibilities included: making local authorities responsible for the long term care of mentally and physically handicapped people in the community; for the long term care of the elderly a single budget financed by the local authority and NHS, under the control of a manager under a joint board; for the mentally ill, either a similar arrangement as proposed for elderly people or assigning all responsibilities to the NHS. What was not tenable, argued the Audit Commission was 'to do nothing about the present financial, organisational and staffing arrangements'.

So community care passed from the accountants to the grocer. The grocer came in the form of Sir Roy Griffiths, the former Managing Director of Sainsburys who had pleased the government earlier in the 1980s with his package of NHS proposals. Norman Fowler asked Griffiths in March 1987 to make a brief review of community care and to advise the Government on how the £6bn. a year could be better utilised.

Sir Roy Griffiths did not formally ask for evidence but it flooded in from statutory, voluntary and private agencies. He liaised with Lady Wagner who had been asked to chair a review of residential care.

In March 1988 the Griffiths report was published 'with a fanfare of muted penny whistles'. (Heptinstall, 1989). In contrast to the earlier publication of the NHS review the Griffiths report received no publicity from the government and was published on budget day at a time when Sir Roy was ill, ensuring that the report was ousted from headline news.

A government silence of 16 months then followed due to the complete unpalatability of the proposals to Mrs Thatcher and to the new Health Minister Kenneth Clarke. What Mrs Thatcher found most distasteful was the major plank of Sir Roy's proposals – that local authorities should take over the lead role in co-ordinating community care. The early and mid-1980s had seen an overt attack on the role and powers of local authorities as manifested in rate capping, abolition of the GLC and other metropolitan authorities, housing and education legislation and to be asked to increase their powers was anathema.

Griffiths' main recommendations were:

1 The designation of a Minister of State responsible for the community care needs of elderly, physically disabled, mentally ill and mentally handicapped adults. The ministerial functions would include preparing and publicising Government's community care objectives and priorities, reviewing local social service authority plans against national objectives, and the allocation of resources.

2 A pivotal role for local social services authorities who should be responsible for assessing the community care needs within their locality and, within the resources available, developing local plans in consultation with health authorities, housing authorities, voluntary bodies and private care providers. The needs of individuals would be identified and assessed, taking full account of their preferences (and those of informal carers). An appropriate package of care would be designed to enable the consumer to live as normal a life as circumstances permit. In effect, SSDs would exchange their present role of providers of care, for that of managing packages of

care provided by different agencies in the public, private, and voluntary sectors.

These two changes would clarify responsibilities and tackle Griffiths' observations that 'community care is a poor relation; everybody's distant relative but nobody's baby'

(Griffiths, 1988).

The need for residential care would be assessed by SSDs who would pay for those unable to meet the costs themselves. This would overcome the 'perverse incentive' identified in the Audit Commission report whereby hard-pressed local social service budgets were eased by people moving into residential care, assisted by payments from central government funds.

Griffiths recommended that the central government funding for community care be 'ring-fenced' or earmarked specifically for that purpose.

Returning to the outcome of the Report – the delay attracted considerable press speculation and caused local authority planning 'blight'. Mrs Thatcher, after heading a Cabinet Committee on community care eventually conceded defeat and in July 1989 the Government announced their broad acceptance of the Griffiths Report but did not agree to 'ring-fencing' money for community care. In November 1989 the White Paper on Community Care was published, followed one week later by the publication of the NHS and Community Care Bill which went through Parliament to become the NHS and Community Care Act 1990.

The White Paper on Community Care 1989

The White Paper defines community care as the provision of 'services and support which people who are affected by problems of ageing, mental illness, mental handicap or physical or sensory disabilities need, to be able to live as independently as possible in their own homes or in 'homely' settings in the community'. The White Paper complements the proposals in the White Paper *Working for Patients* for the management of the hospital and family practitioner services 'Together the two White Papers set out how Government believes Health and Social Care should develop over the next decade'.

The White Paper states that 'the successful implementation of community care policy depends crucially on the availability of and ease of access to adequate and appropriate services in the community'.

The focus of the White Paper is on 'clarifying roles and responsibilities, bringing together the relevant sources of finance, delegating responsibility for decision making to the local level wherever possible, improving accountability and providing the right incentives'.

Promoting choice and independence underlie all the proposals. The White Paper stated that the key components of community care should be:

- services that respond flexibly and sensibly to the needs of individuals and their carers;
- services that allow a range of options for consumers;
- services that intervene no more than is necessary to foster independence;
- services that concentrate on those with the greatest needs.

Six key objectives for service delivery are:

1. Development of domiciliary, day and respite services.
2. To ensure service providers make practical support for carers a high priority.
3. To make proper assessment of need and good case management the cornerstone of high quality care.
4. To promote the development of a flourishing independent sector alongside good quality statutory services.
5. To clarify the responsibilities of agencies to increase performance accountability.
6. To secure better value for money by tackling the problem of 'perverse incentive' towards residential care.

In other words local authorities are to become the key co-ordinators of community care but not necessarily the providers because the private and voluntary sectors are to be encouraged to expand. Yet local authorities' power will increase as they will take over assessment and funding of private residential care to overcome the 'perverse incentive' referred to earlier.

The timetable of changes made to social care delivery and funding as a result of the NHS and Community Care Act 1990

April 91 – (i) Local Authorities (LAs) establish inspection and registration units at arms length from service delivery and set up complaints procedures. *(ii)* Elderly mentally ill people benefit from the requirement of District Health Authorities (DHAs) to introduce community care programmes for those discharged from hospital and from the new specific grant to Local Authorities for services for the mentally ill.

April 92 – LAs publish Community Care Plans to establish clear plans, priorities and targets encompassing: hospital decant policies; the change from service provider to service arranger; the need to ensure services promote independence, sensitivity and choice. Plans must be worked out with health, housing and other authorities tackling the historic difficulties of joint planning and collaboration by focusing on shared values and intended outcomes.

April 93 – *(i)* LAs to be responsible for assessment for social care in collaboration with other agencies where appropriate. Means of referral, criteria for eligibility for assessment and assessment procedures must be publicised. Users' and carers' wishes must be taken into account and there should be only one point of contact for them. Difficulty in separating health and social care needs must be negotiated between health and social services. Careful assessment of elderly people's needs can prevent unnecessary admission to institutional care. *(ii)* LAs set up care/case management systems to enable design to secure delivery of services to meet assessed needs. There should be a clear organisational split between purchaser and provider. LAs will be required to develop a 'mixed economy' of residential, day and domiciliary care for elderly people, utilising the private and voluntary sectors as well as their own direct service providers. They must ensure quality through service specifications in contracts with suppliers. Users may be charged for services. *(iii)* LAs to be responsible for assessing needs of new applicants for public support for residential or nursing home care. It will be the responsibility of the Local Authority to secure a suitable place if residential care is deemed appropriate making maximum use of the independent sector. There will be a financial disincentive against LAs providing residential care directly.

The changes were all originally intended to take place in April 1991 but government anxiety about a £30 per head increase in the already very unpopular poll tax led to the phased programme.

Implementation of the Changes

At the time of writing (November 1992) central government announcements have just been made about the level of funding to be available for the changes in April 1993. Councils in England are to receive £539m, rising to £1,050m in April 1994 and £1,568m in April 1995. Most of the money (£399m) available for April 1993 is a nominal amount which would normally have gone into the government's social security budget to cover people newly entering private or voluntary run residential care. The remaining third (£140m) comes from the Department of Health and is for care management and new home care schemes. Councils have argued that the new money is insufficient for their needs.

The £539m is to be ringfenced after all but not the other £2bn that councils are already spending on community services. To get their share of the new money councils will have to prove they have a strategy with the health service for managing hospital discharges. In addition there are restrictions on how the money is to be used; 75 per cent must be spent on services provided by the independent sector.

A 'Community Care Support Force' has been set up by central government to offer practical support to local authorities and other agencies involved in implementing the community care changes. One reason put forward for the need for this task force and for the restrictions and qualifications surrounding the new community care money is central government's concern with slow progress being made on a number of crucial aspects of the community care changes, notably the continued poor collaboration between NHS & SSDs in some areas and the failure of some SSDs to stimulate the growth of independent sector alternatives to residential care or even to involve the private sector in the preparation of the Community Care Plans that were published in April 1992.

Wardens know at first hand how deeply entrenched is some of the hostility between NHS and SSD staff. GPs are among the most difficult group of workers to involve in multi-disciplinary approaches and their role in the new assessment procedures will be crucial. Central government is issuing a guidance leaflet to all GPs on their role in the community care changes.

The directive to spend three-quarters of the new community care money on the independent sector will only perpetuate existing patterns of care according to the Labour Party. It is argued that the private day and domiciliary sectors are so underdeveloped, councils will be forced to continue to place elderly people in privately-run residential homes.

One aspect of collaboration that has belatedly received government attention is between housing authorities and SSDs. In September 1992 a joint Department of the Environment and

Department of Health Circular called *Housing and Community Care* was issued giving guidance on housing authorities' role in implementing community care. Assessment and planning are two key areas where more joint working is needed.

The circular emphasises that an important element in assessment of individual need is housing need, including adaptations, repairs or improvements. These will require SSDs and housing departments to work co-operatively together and agree referral arrangements so that housing can play its full part in individual assessments.

As with the private sector the evidence is that housing authorities were not fully involved in the drawing up of the Community Care Plans produced by SSDs in April 1992. Perhaps in the revisions to be published in April 1993 greater attention will be paid to the housing aspects of community care.

We encourage wardens to take notice of developments as they are reported in the national press, to find out as much as they can about local changes affecting them and their residents, and to pass their observations on the success or otherwise of the implementation of the changes onto their managers.

Table 3.1 A Summary of the problems of community care in the 1980s and the changes introduced to attempt to solve them

Problems	*Corresponding change*
'Perverse incentive' towards (private) residential care	DSS money to SSDS (April 1993), also full assessment of need
'Organisational fragmentation and confusion'	SSDS – key co-ordinators of community care (April 1993)
Poor planning	SSDS – publish Community Care Plans (April 1992) (in consultation with other agencies)
Complacency by providers and lack of choice to consumers	LA to develop 'mixed economy of care' – promote voluntary and private provisions (April 1992–April 1993)

Neglect of quality of service	Quality control etc. to be built into service contracts
Neglect of complaints procedures	Improved, published systems for customer complaints (April 1991)
Need for greater attention to inspection of establishments	Enhances inspection units (April 1991)
Poor case management	Separation between purchaser and provider; devolved budgets to purchaser; care management systems: requirement to assess, arrange purchase, monitor delivery, ensure detailed service contracts (April 1993)
Inflexible, out-dated home help service	Greater emphasis on targeting a more intensive personal care service to fewer clients. Home Helps → Home carers
Neglect carers	Greater attention to be paid to needs of carers
Lack of resources	Extra funding available though councils say it will not be enough

What about Wardens and the Community Care changes?

The focus of the community care legislation is on change in social services departments and most local authority wardens are employed by housing departments (though Griffiths did suggest that wardens transfer to social services departments, an idea that has not been widely taken up). So what impact will the changes have on wardens and what impact can wardens have on the changes? The second half of that question is the most crucial because of the tendency by SSDs and SSD workers to ignore housing workers and to concentrate any initiatives for collaboration and joint working on the Health Services. We believe that wardens who have a full understanding of the organisation and structure of their local SSD and who have had training in assertiveness should be able to make a significant impact on behalf of their tenants. Some tips are set out below:

1. Act as an advocate/referrer/rereferrer (circumstances and needs change) (see the section in Chapter 5 on advocacy and the end of the section on SSDs in this chapter).
2. Confront/challenge ageism by service providers (see Chapter 5).
3. Contribute to assessment process – ensure accuracy and detail, comprehensive, includes wishes of tenant (see the section on assessment in Chapter 5).
4. Ensure you/your tenants are well informed about services available, confront stigma, ignorance. Use the complaints procedure if necessary. Ensure you and your tenants have copies of the procedure (available from your local SSD).
5. Guard against unnecessary service provision.
6. Ensure carers' needs are not forgotten.
7. Get involved in case conferences (see the section on groups in Chapter 4).
8. Be pro-active in educating other professionals about the potential they have to contribute (e.g. to assessment).
9. Put forward suggestions for improvements in service – your views should be welcomed by own management and those in other agencies.
10. Join with other wardens/other professionals informally via lunch meetings etc.
11. Get involved in allocations if management allows.
12. Contribute your local knowledge to information packs to tenants.
13. Act as consultant on disability/elderly.
14. Tackle NIMBY creatively.
15. Be pro-active and assertive in increasing your knowledge, your involvement and your effectiveness.

Also note that the Audit Commission said successful schemes for Community Care include:

- strong and committed local champions of change;
- a focus on action, not on bureaucratic machinery;
- locally-integrated services cutting across agency boundaries;
- a focus on the local neighbourhood;
- a multi-disciplinary team approach;
- partnership between statutory and voluntary organisations.

It is important to know that the White Paper, Implementation Documents and Circulars all convey that services for elderly people should be: flexible, sensitive, accessible, responsive, personal and targeted on those with greatest need. They should promote: independence, dignity, choice, rights, fulfilment. Clients and their carers should be given clear, jargon-free information on entitlement and availability. In your work you can have these goals for community care to use as tools for own assessment of services. Service providers that fail to live up to these ideals need your feedback and your residents' feedback. The danger of these changes is that front line workers feel alienated from the apparently chaotic and 'topdown' re-organisations and consequently feel overwhelmed, powerless and unimportant. All any warden can do is to continue to chip away in their own small corner at improving the quality of care for their residents.

Residential Care of Older People

Changing Practices

Many wardens have worked in residential care for older people and have made a positive choice to switch to employment in sheltered housing. This is often because residential homes are seen to be depressing places that promote dependence and inhibit choice and dignity in older people. We usually encourage our students to make at least one visit to a 'Part 3' home or similar during the course in order to see if practices and attitudes have changed.

Residential care used to be seen as a last resort for older people, many of whom remember tales of the horrors of the workhouse. Research, scandals and changing attitudes have contributed to a more positive approach by professionals to the provision of residential care. We are encouraged to see such care as offering refuge, rehabilitation, support and stimulation and not as just a place for custody or basic care services.

More attention is paid now to the need for careful assessment, allocation and admission procedures. Prospective residents and their families need to be involved in all stages of their application and to be offered preliminary visits and trial periods before giving up existing accommodation.

The provision of material comfort is important as well as the opportunity for the resident to exercise their choice over their surroundings. These days double occupancy rooms are frowned on and efforts have been made to offer more single rooms with residents' choice of decor and the opportunity to bring personal belongings and perhaps a favourite chair. Small homes offering up to 20 places are increasingly preferred over the large scale 50+ type of home. Some large homes have adapted to changing policies by the use of group living schemes whereby residents live and identify with a small section of the total number.

Goals

Homes are encouraged to state their goals or aims and objectives in clear and precise terms. These are often set out in a brochure for prospective residents and their families. Procedures for complaints should also be publicised. Key goals of homes should be the promotion of dignity, respect, privacy, independence and choice. The home's policy on the balance of safety with risk taking should also be made clear.

From these values and goals good practice should follow. Examples include: staff showing respectful attitudes towards the residents regarding mode of address and entering bedrooms; choice of meals, clothes, bathtimes, bedtimes, mealtimes, social activities; dignity regarding toileting and bathing; recognition of each individual's needs and wishes bearing in mind ethnic, religious and cultural differences. An excellent guide to good practice in residential care is given in the references at the end of this Chapter (Avebury, 1984).

Wardens can utilise their earlier and more recent experience of working and/or visiting homes in their locality by accompanying residents on visits and advising those residents who are considering a move to residential accommodation. Families and tenants can be alerted by the warden to the changing philosophy in residential care, and helped to look out for examples of good practice in homes they choose to visit.

Home Care

Home care is clearly a part of community care but because of its significance to many sheltered housing residents we have given it a separate section.

Changes

Depending on how long you have been a warden and on the area where you work you may well have seen major changes in the way your local authority runs its home help or home care service. These changes are likely to have affected your tenants and caused some controversy. This section aims to explain the background and nature of these changes and to consider their implications for you, the tenants and their relatives.

In a nutshell, many home help services have changed from providing a service that is primarily domestic (cleaning) to a 'targeted' personal care service. As we have seen there has been an increased central government emphasis on the need to provide services to help people to remain in their own homes and an increasing number of frail elderly people living at home. At the same time there has been concern with waste and inefficiency in the home help service (eight home helps queueing for pensions at the same time in one post office, a quarter of home help time in one area spent in trudging to and from shops). Many government reports have commented on the inflexible high coverage, low intensity service available in the traditional home help service. Statistics have shown that the allocation of time is not consistent with authorities intentions to support highly dependent people.

Innovations that have happened as a consequence of these pressures on the home help service include:

- changing the name from home help to home care service;
- ending cleaning only service (in some authorities for existing clients as well as for new ones causing considerable uproar);
- increased personal care (bathing, washing, catheter bag emptying, putting to bed);
- more flexible hours offered including night sitting;
- more support to informal carers;
- shopping schemes;
- more careful assessment and targeting, reviews and reassessments;
- more careful objectives spelt out for the service against which success can be measured;
- better trained staff;
- better links with private sector, health service, voluntary organisations.

Some Solutions to the Problems

Some authorities have published accounts of the changes they have made to the home care service, identifying problems they met and giving some of their solutions to them. Tips they have given that are of relevance to you as wardens include:

- if a service is to be stopped, staff must know where to direct users to get an alternative service (e.g. give guidance to clients on where to get a private cleaner);
- value old skills as well as train in new ones;
- involve all levels of staff in consultation processes and in workshops to encourage innovation and secure commitment at all levels;
- consult with other agencies early on e.g. demarcation lines of tasks between nursing and caring staff;
- combine roles of home help with nursing auxiliary or domiciliary aid with domiciliary nurse;
- ensure carers and users views are heard in the planning process;
- consider contracts for formal and informal carers;
- ensure only newcomers to the service are effected by a change in policy since a long established relationship between a client and a home help providing a traditional domestic service may provide unmeasurable preventive, social and therapeutic benefits.

In addition many of our comments on assessment in Chapter 5 are relevant here and the section in this chapter on the Private Sector.

Day Care

Types

As with the home help service there have been changes in day care facilities in recent years though they have been less dramatic. Before examining these changes and some current issues it is worth clarifying the four main types of provision.

1. Day hospitals composed of geriatric day hospitals for short-term treatment and rehabilitation where attendance should be time-limited, and psychogeriatric day hospitals with no time limit on attendance, providing both short-term and long-term care.
2. SSD community-based day centres.
3. SSD day care-residential homes.
4. Voluntary community-based day centres.

In your own area you may have all four types of day centre on offer or only one or two. The centres may be multi-purpose, catering for several client groups or they may cater for one group only.

Day care has been neglected as an area for research and development and consumers views often not sought or heard. The community care legislation should in theory change this as responding to consumers' views is a central requirement.

Why Day Care?

When referring someone for day care consider why, what is the purpose. If the principle reason is for company consider other day facilities which may be less stigmatising and less ghettoising of older people, e.g. educational classes, sports activities, political groups etc. Reflect on your own ageism if these hadn't occurred to you!

Quality

Find out about all the local day care services in your area. Your wide knowledge can be a real asset to your tenants and to other professionals who may tend to assess narrowly according to their own agency and its services. Research has shown that the type of service received often depends on which agency or professional is involved, so that elderly people do not always get the service most suited to their needs. And it is often difficult for people to move between types of unit especially from day hospital to day centre.

Find out about what actually goes on in the local day centres. Get copies of the stated aims and objectives of them and compare these to what you actually observe. Research has shown that despite often laudable objectives a comparatively low proportion of users' time, even in days hospitals, is spent in therapeutic activities.

Susan Tester in her research for the Centre for Policy on Ageing concluded that there needs to be greater clarity in defining day care services and their purposes. Their aims are diverse and sometimes conflicting or not clearly stated. It is often assumed that day care will reduce loneliness but increased social contacts may not necessarily produce the close relationships needed to relieve loneliness. There are other social, leisure and educational facilities which older people could attend.

> We find the association between older age, loneliness and day care services are unhelpful. It seems to advocate that older people should be taken out of normal community life and receive their social contacts in separate places.
>
> (Tester, 1988).

Tester recommends day care services be distinguished from day facilities. Day care services would focus firstly on short-term social and medical assessment, treatment, rehabilitation and therapy and secondly on longer-term maintenance, monitoring and relief for carers. Day facilities would be for those whose main needs are for company including day and lunch clubs, education and leisure facilities, libraries, sports centres.

We now turn to our second approach to analysing services, namely according to the nature of the provider.

Statutory Providers of Care for Older People

Social Services Departments

Currently most local authority wardens are employed by the housing department and not the SSD. Consequently most wardens are rather uninformed about the background, organisation, functions and scope of SSDs. In some cases this lack of knowledge is combined with resentment or even hostility, perhaps two-way. On our course we seek to address this both in class discussion and through visits organised by the students. We find that, armed with some basic information about SSDs and energised by the increased feelings of self-confidence that the course brings, students are often able to make an effective link with their peers and colleagues in SSDs. Bridges are built, misinformation and misunderstandings on both sides are cleared up and working relationships improve dramatically, especially necessary now with the community care changes.

So what is this basic information that wardens need to know about SSDs? We usually ask the students to tell us what puzzles or interests them about SSDs and the rest of this section is based on their questions and our 'answers'.

What are the origins of SSDs and of Social Work?

To provide simple answers to these questions it is necessary to refer to the development of social policy in the nineteenth century, in particular the setting up of the Charity Organisation Society (COS) in 1869 in response to the harsh social conditions at that time. The 1834 Poor Law (Amendment) Act had imposed great hardships on many people who were destitute through no fault of their own. The COS was very active in working with poor people and in a variety of ways, including group, community and case work. Local authorities took over the administration of the Poor Law in 1929 absorbing some voluntary activity too, and in the post war 'welfare state' reforms the basis of the scope of our modern day SSD was set up, albeit in separate departments for children (Children's Department), old and disabled people (Welfare Department), mentally ill and mentally handicapped people (Health Department) until 1970 following the recommendations of the Seebohm report in 1968 and its implementation in the Local Authority Social Services Act 1970.

Social work, which is of course a key activity provided by SSDs, therefore has its roots in the twin philosophies of social control (Poor Law) and social welfare (COS). To this day these two aspects of social work make uneasy bedfellows.

Social workers became a more united and cohesive group of workers from the early 1970s and worked in a more 'generic' (general) way than pre-1970 when they had been very specialised according to client group.

What has Happened to SSDs and Social Work with Older People Since 1970?

There have been many controversies, some public, some internal, in the personal social services. A key issue has been the failure of SSDs to become the 'fifth social service' that Seebohm had envisaged. SSDs were to become 'family-orientated, community based, available and accessible to all'. Economic and political changes in the 1970s together with increased public interest and concern in the value of social work following the Maria Colwell scandal in 1974 meant that this never happened. SSDs remain a stigmatising service provider mostly for poor people.

Another key issue is the generic versus specialist debate referred to earlier. Older people were said to have lost out in the Seebohm reforms due to the ending of specialist work with them. Generic social workers appeared to favour and prioritise work with children and work with older people was seen as less demanding, less prestigious and requiring the attentions of less qualified or unqualified staff.

The implementations of the recommendations of the Barclay Report 1982 *The Role of and Tasks of Social Workers* further exacerbated this trend via the emphasis on patch or neighbourhood teams.

The changes under the NHS and Community Care Act 1990 will in some ways turn the clock back as we are seeing a return to specialism with some social workers concentrating on work with children and the rest focusing on work with adults.

Who Can Get Help From SSDs?

A vast number of Acts of Parliament have determined the scope and duties of SSDs. Some of these powers are mandatory, some permissive. In times of economic difficulty local authorities prioritise only the key mandatory statutory work with the main client groups. These are children (especially child abuse, fostering and adoption), people with mental illness (including 'sectioning' people into a psychiatric hospital) or mental handicap/learning difficulty, people with physical disabilities, older people, young offenders.

What Sort of Help do SSDs Give and Where?

Sometimes the help provided is divided into five types determined by setting: fieldwork, community work, domiciliary care, day care, residential care. Another framework might be by client group (see above section) and a third might be by methods (case, group or community work). Using the first system of classification, field work includes visits by social workers, social work assistants and occupational therapists to people's own homes, usually for assessment, sometimes for ongoing casework. Community work is both a setting and a method and is referred to below under the third framework by method.

A key aspect of domiciliary care is referred to in the separate section on Home Care Service. The other crucial domiciliary care service is meals on wheels. Our students have found the opportunity to research and study this topic in depth surprisingly rewarding. Issues of nutrition, rationing, low take up, provision for ethnic minority elderly people and preventable dependence are all fascinating to explore.

Day care and residential care have their own sections in this chapter.

Returning to the framework of analysing help by methods of intervention, casework is the most central method. Key skills used by the social worker here are listening, counselling, assessment, support, negotiation, advocacy – very similar in fact to the skills that wardens utilise and have the opportunity of developing on the NWCC. Group work builds on these skills and also demands specialist knowledge of how groups work and skills in the facilitation of groups. Community work requires a focus on the needs of the community as a whole rather than on the needs of individuals.

Who Works For SSDs and How Are They Structured?

As well as qualified social workers there may also be unqualified social workers, social work assistants, social work aids, specialist advisers for the blind or deaf, occupational therapists. With the community care changes we will see a 'new breed' called case or care manager as well as the usual team leaders, senior social workers, area team managers. It is impossible to provide a typical structure now of a SSD, so great is the range of possibilities following major restructuring concurrent with the phased implementation of the NHS and Community Care Act 1990. All wardens are encouraged to request an organisation chart of their local SSD from the Head Office and to make contact with strategic people in their local area.

How Do I Get Help from SSDs?

Sadly, this question is often expressed in terms of despair or cynicism by wardens on our course. The referral process is in theory quite straightforward necessitating a simple phone call to the local area team. The receptionist puts you through to the duty social worker if the case is unknown or closed, or to the regular social worker if the case is open. Therein lies the rub – most 'elderly cases' are not kept open for regular ongoing support or supervision by SSDs these days. Priority for allocations is given only to emergency or at risk cases due to the failure of SSDs' staffing and other resourcing to keep up with increasing demands. All very rational and efficient for the service provider but for users and referrers these rationing decisions can sometimes seem harsh, unfair and even inexplicable (see the section on rationing at the end of this chapter).

Our advice to wardens when attempting to refer someone to social services is to be very precise with your facts about the case, giving examples of behaviour or incidents that back up your view that, say, the person is at risk and/or that their behaviour is extremely challenging (see section on assessment in Chapter 5). Be prepared to calmly explain the story two or three times and to emphasise key aspects. Be clear in what you are asking of the SSD and when you feel this action needs to be taken by. Emphasise the contribution you have made and can continue to make to the management of the case and to the full assessment process. Explain the limitations of your own role.

All this is usually done verbally over the phone to the duty officer. Back it up with a letter if you think it will help. Chase it up with a letter anyway if the response is not forthcoming. Agencies find letters harder to ignore or forget about than phone calls.

National Health Service

The Changes in the NHS

The NHS has been brought to a crucial stage in its history. It is facing an enormous set of challenges as a result of various re-organisations over the last 20 years.

Two decades have seen changes in the organisation and structure of the NHS, in its management and administration and recently the introduction of moneterist principles to its operating basis. Hand-in-hand with these reforms has gone a cultural change.

Professional staff have become managers in a more formal and structured way. For example Matrons have become Directors of Nursing Services, Nursing Officers have become Nurse Managers and Sisters/Charge Nurses have become Ward Managers. More recently lay managers or general managers have been recruited to direct the work of health care professionals.

The reasons given for change in the NHS have been to minimise waste, save money, re-allocate resources to maximise service delivery (reducing administrators and managers to increase 'front-line' or hands-on care workers). However, subtle shifts have occurred. Enabling care staff to see the prices of what they used during their work led to formal systems that put a price on every item. This then led to the introduction of budgets that care staff managed. It is now very common for the managers of wards and departments to have a budget allocation within which they must remain. Inevitably conflicts have arisen between the sum allocated and the cost of treatments, etc.

Managers are therefore forced to set limits on the work of health care staff to conform to the aims of senior managers. A White Paper *Promoting Better Health* (1987) placed an emphasis on health promotion and disease prevention, new contracts for General Practitioners (effected April 1990) and Dentists (effected October 1990).

The GP contract makes provision for health checks on all new patients, three yearly checks on patients who have not been seen in that period and annual checks on all patients of 75 years and older.

Another White Paper *Working for Patients* (1989) was intended to examine the management and funding of the NHS. Contractual funding arose from this White Paper and is the method underpinning the NHS and Community Care Act 1990 which gave the government powers to create the NHS Trust hospitals and units. Some essential and basic changes have been made within the Act to the way the NHS has been run since 1948 when it came into existence.

Basically a NHS Trust is obliged to 'compete' with other providers of health care for contracts with the District Health Authorities (DHAs) and Fundholding GPs.

Health authorities will purchase care on behalf of their catchment population from these 'providers'. The DHA now has to identify the health needs of its client population and bid for funds from the Regional Health Authority (or Department of Health directly).

The DHA then looks to the 'health care market' to buy the care from NHS Trusts, private hospitals, units still within the NHS (DMU – Directly Managed Unit), etc.

Additionally, doctors and nurses have been given greater responsibilities for the day-to-day management of staff and resources.

The Regional and District Health Authorities have also been restructured. Much of the power to determine health care strategy has been placed with those managing the care units (hospitals, GPs etc).

The effect on GPs will be that some practices (over 9000 patients) will be able to hold their own budgets or funds for a limited number of services and their prescriptions. This budget will be set by the Regional Health Authority and deducted from the sum allocated to the DHA covering that practice.

General practioners who do not hold budgets will be set a prescribing budget. This will be set and monitored by the Family

Health Services Authority (FHSA). The FHSA will also monitor the spending of Fundholding GPs against the sum deducted from the DHA budget.

At the time of writing there are many controversies surrounding these changes including so called 'gagging' contracts for trust staff, redundancies and reduced services. A major unresolved problem is the lack of agreement between central government, the NHS and local government over which agency is responsible for the funding and provision of care for the long-term sick elderly.

Wardens will need to become even more assertive in negotiating with GPs and hospitals on behalf of their tenants and to be very well informed about local services and options available.

Private Sector for Older People

Many wardens and indeed many other professionals working for the public or voluntary sectors are suspicious of the private sector and of those working in it. With a changing political climate we are not doing our clients a favour if we keep our heads in the sand. We need to familiarise ourselves with the range of private services available and developing in our areas, yet remain alert to the possible problems of increased reliance on private care.

One of the main intentions of the current community care changes is to promote the development of the private or independent sector. SSDs were obliged to spell out their plans for generating and encouraging private sector provision of services in their Community Care Plans published in April 1992 and, as we explained earlier in this chapter, 85 per cent of the new money available from April 1993 must be spent on the independent sector.

The idealised picture that is portrayed of the private sector is drawn from the relatively organised worlds of business and industry. These operate on the basis of much factual evidence of their financial and other activities. The SSDs will struggle to plan and promote the independent sector with the fragmented and sparse information available to them.

Added to the problem of inadequate data is the failure of the private sector to relate its services to need. The geographical spread of private residential homes is most uneven, with inner London, for example, considerably underprovided for. In the domiciliary sector there is evidence of private agencies' reluctance to offer personal care to the most dependent frail or challenging older people, leaving this group to the statutory services.

We shall look now at some specific issues relating to two of the three main types of private care, residential and domiciliary. Private sheltered housing was looked at in Chapter 2.

Private residential care for older people

The private residential care sector is highly fragmented and is only partially organised under representative bodies. Local authorities vary in the success of their attempts at communication with these bodies and their members. The sector remains secretive about matters such as staffing ratios or training making monitoring and regulation harder than it might be. The April 1993 changes referred to in the section on the NHS and Community Care Act 1990 whereby Local Authority Social Service Departments will assess new referrals to private homes are in part intended to avoid the inappropriate admissions to homes that have been so draining of public expenditure. However, the stipulation that 85 per cent of the new money for community care should be spent on the independent sector has raised concerns that this old pattern will continue in the absence of sufficient private sector day or domiciliary care.

Private domiciliary care for older people

The use of private domestic help has tended to be by the least needy – i.e. the better off, younger elderly and elderly couples. Most private domestic work is carried out by self employed part-time female workers and is therefore disorganised and unregulated. Similarly the private agencies also tend to lack systems for regulation and inspection. Perhaps individual domestic workers will become more regulated by the introduction of a local authority system comparable to that for child minders. But the authorities have no such model to assist with the development of quality control systems for the agencies.

There may be opportunity for expansion for the private entrepreneur in the areas of respite care, assessment, resettlement of ex-hospital patients, daily care centres.

Wardens are encouraged to keep their eyes and ears open to

developments in the private sector in their areas to be able to advise tenants and other professionals alike.

The Voluntary Sector

This includes both voluntary organisations or agencies and volunteers. Voluntary agencies, such as Age Concern, are run and financed as charitable or non-profit making organisations and are not technically part of local or central government. In practice many voluntary organisations are not in fact independent of the state because they rely on government grants to survive. Many workers in voluntary agencies are paid though many are unpaid volunteers. Your local Age Concern and Help the Aged are likely to be staffed by a complex mixture of paid and unpaid staff. The Age Concern movement is the country's second largest provider (after the NHS) of services to older people.

As with the private sector, the current community care changes are intended to promote and develop the use of voluntary sector provision of care for older people. The voluntary sector is said to have certain characteristics in its favour – notably that it widens consumer choice, provides for specialised needs, is cost-effective, is flexible and innovative, promotes greater consumer participation and speaks up for client groups. Are these qualities apparent in your local voluntary agencies? You could perhaps compare two day centres in your local area, one run by the SSD and one run by Age Concern or Help the Aged and decide whether the voluntary centre rates higher on these criteria than the statutory one.

The community care changes require local authorities to make the arrangements between them and voluntary agencies more formalised in the form of contracts. Some research by the Association of County Councils in the late 1980s suggested that at that time only 12 per cent of councils had made formal contracts for care with voluntary organisations.

Some reservations have been expressed about both the enhanced role of the voluntary sector and the contractual climate needed to achieve it. These include a fear that the larger, more established voluntary organisations will be favoured by local authorities who will prefer to arrange contracts with a few organisations, not lots of small ones. Another concern is that the need to comply with regulations such as fire and registration will increase costs and alter the philosophy of some organisations. The autonomy of agencies may be endangered, yet meaningful consultation by local authorities may continue to be lacking.

Voluntary agencies have always suffered from financial insecurity and, for some, the changes may not help at all.

Family Care of Older People

Extent

Most care of the elderly is provided either by themselves or by their families. In recent years there has been much influential research documenting the extent, duration and nature of this care and statistics are quoted on how much money is saved through the free care provided by families (£15bn. to £24bn. a year). Fifty-seven per cent of the six million carers cannot get a two-day break, one-third have children and one-half have jobs. Fifty-eight per cent of carers have their own health problems. A pressure group the 'Carers National Association' was formed in 1981 and has successfully raised public awareness of the existence and plight of the six million people who provide unpaid care. Television and radio programmes, training courses and publications have all sought in recent years to help the carer become less isolated, more assertive and more knowledgeable about benefits and services available. Feminists have been influential in highlighting the extent to which unpaid care has been predominately provided by women (though two and one-half million of the six million carers are now men) encouraging policy makers and professionals to challenge their sexist assumptions that this should continue to be the case. The range of benefits available to dependent elderly people and their carers has been increased though not sufficient to meet the wide range of needs.

Warden's Role

Wardens tend to work with elderly people who are unrepresentative of elderly people as a whole and this can distort their impressions of elderly people's families. People who go into sheltered housing tend to have no family or come from families who are less able or less willing to provide care than those elderly people who remain in the community. The attraction of the warden service to some families is that the warden can provide the daily contact that the family cannot or will not. Families able and willing to provide such support themselves do not need to encourage their relatives to go into sheltered housing. Wardens need to come to terms with this fact of life of sheltered housing and to work creatively and constructively with families within these constraints. Relatives often have conflicting emotions towards the elderly person and wardens can help by listening, supporting and advising. Listening to and acknowledging the guilt, anger, grief often associated with caring for an increasingly frail elderly person requires skill, patience and efforts to be non-judgemental (see section on counselling skills in Chapter 4). Wardens can explain the symptoms and stages of dementia to relatives offering reassurance and advice about other services available. Carers need to be encouraged not to become guilt-ridden martyrs but to keep their own lives, hobbies and interests going and growing. Wardens can also help carers come to terms with the elderly person going into residential care where appropriate and can help achieve an outcome of 'positive choice'.

The problems that carers face can be summarised as:

- psychological – the effects of relentless 24-hour care on the emotions and mental health;
- physical – strenuous lifting and bathing can harm the physical health of the carer;
- social isolation and lack of recognition;
- financial problems – due to loss of income if a paid job is given up, inadequate compensation in state benefits;
- lack of practical support – cuts in services have led to priority being given to those with no relatives.

Wardens can share an assessment of the carer's needs, perhaps analysed in the form outlined above, with service providers, case managers or social workers. The NHS and Community Care Act 1990 places, as we have seen, an obligation on SSDs to take carers' needs into account. See the sections on assessment (Chapter 5) and SSDs (this chapter) for further guidance on assessment and referral of carers who should be seen as clients in their own right.

Rationing of Services

Throughout this book we refer to services for older people and to the needs that they are there to meet. We will address here the process by which the two are reconciled, in other words rationing or 'the process by which a limited resource is divided between various competing bodies' (Scrivens, 1979).

When we need clothes or food we use money to purchase them. Demand and supply are balanced by price, but access to social services, up until very recently, has been determined by need, not ability to pay. However, as supply has not kept pace with demand, other ways of balancing the two have had to be used. These other ways are called rationing techniques, whereby need or demand are controlled, reduced, deflected or diluted. These processes are often not explicit and open but implicit and hidden.

Demand Controllers The waiting list is a popular method of controlling demand but has to be used in conjunction with other rationing methods if lists become very long and people have to wait an inappropriate length of time before a service is available to them.

Rigorous criteria of eligibility for a service are often devised as an effective way of controlling demand. When the supply of a service decreases (due to cuts) and/or demand increases (perhaps due to demographic changes) the criteria can be tightened or narrowed. Cynically this can be called 'moving the goalposts' by unfortunate potential service users who are denied the service under new rules. Home care services are a classic example.

In favour of the above two methods of controlling demand it can be said that they are at least explicit and available for potential users to read and understand. The same cannot be said for our third demand controller – professional assessment of need. All too often this is used inconsistently, arbitrarily and in such a way as to render the client powerless and without redress. Professional assessments of need can mystify and intimidate the user and may even negate the other more explicit rationing mechanisms. An example of this in some areas is Part 3 admissions. The waiting list may be so long that people are dead by the time they come to the top of them through queuing. The eligibility criteria may be too broad so allow access to the list to unrealistic numbers of people. So the way that places may be allocated to Part 3 may be entirely on the basis of social workers arguing that their own individual client is a priority, a special, urgent or emergency case. Some local authorities have made attempts to rigorously analyse priorities and make the criteria for eligibility more explicit. Customers may not like being turned down but at least they know the rules.

Demand reducers Regrettably many older people are now not applying for essential services because of their costs. The new charging bands for various packages of home care may not be intended to reduce demand but this can be their effect. Many older people may also be deterred from asking for a service out of pride or shame or wish to remain independent and not receive 'charity'. If the service-providers take no steps to acknowledge these processes and to creatively challenge hints of stigma in the application and referral process then demand continues to be, perhaps unintentionally, reduced. Services with means tests always have a lower take up than those without. Older people in particular resent the stigmatising connotations of them. Many of us, even professionals working within the welfare state, have only a hazy or incomplete knowledge of the full range of services available for older people. There are variations between local authorities and even within them. Some older people may misunderstand their entitlement to a service or have misconceptions about the nature of it in the first place. Take-up may therefore be lowered especially if the provider does not advertise its services.

If the procedure for obtaining a service is complex this can deter an applicant from applying, as can the knowledge that a previous claim was turned down.

The ageism of some professionals or even potential applicants can reduce demand. The attitudes 'What does she expect at her age?' referred in the section on ageism in Chapter 5 has been convenient to many services in keeping expectations on the low side.

Demand deflectors When there are considerable pressures on us and our time as individuals we are inclined to metaphorically put blinkers on and concentrate on what we know we have to do. We can be tempted to 'pass the buck' onto someone else. Organisations are no different and in particular the agencies providing services for older people. Health, housing and social service departments can define an elderly person's problems and needs narrowly and then argue that they therefore are not their responsibility but another agencies'. For clients, their health, housing and social needs are not so easily distinguished and they may be pushed backwards and forwards between reluctant providers of services. All this is supposed to change with the NHS and Community Care Act 1990 when assessment becomes a key responsibility of SSDs and the client is supposed to receive a seam-free service. At the time of writing there appears to be a long way to go before this goal is achieved.

Demand Diluters The quantity or quality of the service may be reduced. Quantity can be reduced for example by changing the number of home help hours per week that a customer receives from four to two per week. Quality can be reduced by passing all work of a certain type onto untrained staff where previously trained staff were used.

Access to Services

The NHS and Community Care Act 1990 emphasises that services should be accessible to those who need them. Service providers are encouraged to identify and modify all those aspects of the referral process that inhibit access. The physical position and layout of the local office may be off-putting. Perhaps the location could be changed so the office is in a high street or on popular bus routes. Perhaps ramps are needed or the reception area needs to be made more welcoming. The receptionist is crucially important and acts as a 'gatekeeper' to professionals and hence services. Training in customer relations is much more common nowadays as there is more recognition of the role of front line staff.

Attention needs to be given to the needs of non-English speaking or reading potential customers and also to the sensory-impaired. Translations, interpreters, braille and loop systems all need to be evaluated and costed into the service.

References and Further Reading

Audit Commission (1986) *Making a Reality of Community Care* London: HMSO.

Avebury, Lady K (1984) *Home Life: A Code of Practice for Residential Care* London: Centre for Policy on Ageing.

Barclay P (1982) *Social Workers: Role and Tasks* London: Bedford Square Press.

Butler A and Pritchard C (1983) *Social Work and Mental Illness* London: Macmillan Press Ltd.

Department of the Environment/Department of Health (1992) Joint circular *Housing in Community Care* London: HMSO.

Family Policy Studies Centre (1991) *An Ageing Population* Fact Sheet 2 London: Family Policy Studies Centre.

Froggatt A (1990) *Family Work with Elderly People* Basingstoke: Macmillan Education Ltd.

Griffiths R (1988) *Community Care: Agenda for Action* London: HMSO.

Heptinstall D (1989) At the end of the Journey in *Social Work Today* 27 July 1989 p16–17 (on the background to the community care changes).
HMSO (1992) *Leaving Hospital: Elderly People and their Discharge to Community Care* London: HMSO.
Kirk H and Leather P (1991) *Age File: The Facts* Oxford: Anchor Housing Trust.
Marshall M (ed) (1990) *Working with Dementia* Birmingham: Venture Press.
National Health Service and Community Care Act (1990) London HMSO.
Scrivens E (1979) Towards a Theory of Rationing in *Social Policy and Administration* Vol 13, No 1 Spring 1979.
Stevenson O (1989) *Age and Vulnerability, A guide to better care* London: Edward Arnold.
Tester S (1989) *Caring by Day: a study of day care services for older people* London: Centre for Policy on Ageing.
Thane P (1987) Golden Oldies in *New Society* 13 November 1989 pp12–13.
West S (1992) *Your Rights 1992–92 – A Guide to money benefits for Older People* London: Age Concern, England.
White Paper (1987) *Promoting Better Health* London: HMSO.
White Paper (1989) *Working for Patients* London: HMSO.
White Paper (1989) *Caring for People: Community Care into the Next Decade and Beyond* (Cmmd 849) London: HMSO.

PART 2
Skills and good practice issues for wardens

CHAPTER 4
Communication Skills

Introduction

An undervalued aspect of the warden's job is the need for skilled communication. Without attention to this, mistakes are made, misunderstandings occur and neglect can arise.

Wardens communicate on a one-to-one basis with tenants, professionals etc. – orally on the phone and face-to-face or in writing by report, memo or letter. They communicate with groups – families, tenants. Perhaps because communication is such an everyday, taken-for-granted activity the successful communicator is rarely noticed. Yet, like housework not done, failure to communicate does get noticed and bad feelings can follow. In this chapter we will look in turn at each of the component parts of communication skills. The chapters that follow utilise and develop some of these core skills. We will begin this chapter with an outline of the key aspects of oral communication; listening, questioning and assertiveness. An overview of the further skills of counselling, stress management and working in groups follows. We have included a section on reminiscence work here as this also requires group work skills. Finally, in this chapter we will look at the written skill of report writing.

Listening

Listening is the core skill in communicating but is something we are not taught as it is assumed to be common sense. Yet nearly everyone we have ever trained in listening and counselling skills has told us how surprised they were when doing the class exercises to find that *good* listening is hard. In fact listening is an exercise in self-restraint. When we listen to someone we must avoid interrupting, judging or imposing ourself on the speaker.

Try this exercise with a trusted friend or colleague:

One speaks for two minutes about something important to them while the other JUST LISTENS.

After two minutes the listener then feeds back to the speaker what was said. The speaker then says whether this was accurate.

Then reverse (i.e. speaker becomes listener).

Afterwards, ask yourselves – what did you each notice when you were listening? What distracted you from giving your complete attention (e.g. identification, disagreement, embarrassment etc.).

Listening is not just the absence of speaking and remaining silent – it is a highly skilled and purposeful activity. The beauty of recognising our weaknesses when listening is what we can then work on correcting them in ordinary daily life – thereby improving the quality of the attention we give people and at the same time our own job satisfaction.

Some aids to good listening include:

This is an active process

Be prepared to listen:	– think about what the speaker is saying, not what you'll say next.
Be interested:	– the listener has equal responsibility for communication;
	– make appropriate responses – look interested;
	– look for ideas you can use; relate what's said to your situation (but see 'Hold Back' below).
Be open minded:	– be aware of your own prejudices – don't let them get in the way.
Listen for main ideas:	– not just facts – but also ideas and/or emotions behind facts;
	– be alert to the main points of the message.
Listen critically:	– but in an unbiased way;
	– weigh up the value of the evidence/basis of the logic behind the message.
Resist distractions:	– concentrate, don't switch off/glaze over.
Help the speaker:	– give appropriate responses – verbal and physical;
	– 'yes' 'I see' etc.;
	– nodding, appropriate body language.

Playback/reflective listening:
- ask speaker to elaborate a point;
- 'echo' remarks made by the speaker to show speaker you were really listening and to offer encouragement to go on and to check you have really understood.

Hold back:
- don't interrupt;
- allow silences/pauses.

Benefits of listening:

Encouragement to others:
- non threatening listening helps others to lose their defensiveness
- in return they understand you better by listening more effectively to you.

Possession of all the information:
- we need as much relevant information as possible to make decisions/solve problems. Careful listening will motivate the continued giving of facts.

Improved relationships:
- gives speaker the opportunity to get:
  - facts
  - ideas
  - hostile feelings off her/his chest
  - speaker appreciates your interest.

Resolution of problems:
- disagreements and problems can best be solved when individuals listen carefully to one another – not necessarily *agree* with one another – but understand the other's point of view.
- everyone needs understanding – this can be expressed through effective listening.
- talking through a problem can help us mutually to work out possible solutions.

Better Understanding of People:
- careful listening to others will give clues as to how they think, what they think is important and why they are saying what is being said.
- understanding others help us work with them and lead to greater harmony.

Questioning

Following on from the need for good quality listening is the need to ask appropriately-phrased questions. Once again we are not taught how to ask questions – it is assumed to be common sense and that only specialists like personnel managers and other professional interviewers need to learn techniques.

Yet everyone including wardens can benefit from understanding and applying good question techniques.

Closed Questions vs. Open Questions

Closed questions beginning with 'Do you . . .?' get yes or no answers and do not elicit much more than this unless combined with the more open 'Tell me about . . .?' in which the speaker is actively encouraged to tell their story in their own way, in their own words, without a structure imposed by the questioner's limiting and closed questions, e.g. rather than 'Do you live here because your husband died?' ask 'Tell me about how you came to live here'.

Leading Questions

Often we frame questions in such a way that we get the answer we want to hear e.g. 'Do you like living here?' or 'Have you settled in now?' These are called leading questions and are probably the easiest and commonest mistake made by people untrained in questioning. We delude ourselves that we are being reassuring or caring yet we are often just trying to reassure ourselves not open ourselves to the possibility of another person's pain or risk receiving an answer we do not want to hear. So we ask the closed leading question, 'Are you feeling better today Mrs Simpson?' rather than the open 'How are you feeling today Mrs Simpson?' or 'Did you have a good holiday?' rather than 'What sort of holiday did you have?' We can impose our own feelings onto another person by insensitive question techniques, and by jumping to conclusions, prevent the other person telling their own story or sharing their own feelings in their own way. For example, (closed leading) 'Are you feeling okay about going into hospital next week?' instead of 'How are you feeling about going into hospital next week?'

Multiple Questions

We can sometimes make matters even worse by asking multiple questions (which may or may not also be leading) such as 'Do you like it at the luncheon club, have you been going long and made some nice friends?' This confuses the other person who is not sure what part to answer and may not even remember all the parts. They may also sense that the question is somehow insincere or patronising and not be inclined to share their thoughts and feelings in response.

Counselling

This section will explain what counselling is and is not, and what qualities and skills are used in counselling situations. It will not train you as a counsellor since this has to be done over a long period of time and face-to-face – no one can ever become a counsellor from reading a book. Yet we have found that just an increased awareness of the techniques used in counselling has enlightened our students and has helped them become clearer about their role, its boundaries, possibilities and limitations.

Not Advice Giving

We usually begin a teaching session on counselling by brainstorming the word. Invariably the phrase 'giving advice' crops up and this indicates the most common and fundamental misconception about counselling which is that the counsellor suggests or imposes their solutions on the client. The person using counselling techniques in fact does the opposite by trying to create a safe, relaxed climate for the client in which she can work out her own solutions, arrive at her own decisions. The counsellor resists totally the temptation to say 'if I were you I would . . .' or 'when I was in that situation I did . . .'

Listening and Questioning

The counsellor uses active listening as the main skill and in particular listens for clues as to the feelings associated with the client's story. Open questions are used to draw the client out or reflective statements are used to encourage them to elaborate. See the earlier sections in this chapter on listening and questioning. This example illustrates these points:

Client: 'My husband died 5 years ago'.
Counsellor: 'Can you tell me how you feel' or 'You sound sad when you say that'. (This statement is an example of 'reflecting back'.)

NOT 'You must be lonely' or 'Yes my husband died last year so I know how you feel'.

Client-centred not Counsellor-centred

The correct use of counselling techniques keeps the focus entirely on the client and does not impose the counsellor's experiences, feelings or views. Ordinary conversation is two-way in which both parties attempt to get their needs met. In counselling the needs of the client are paramount and the counsellor must get her needs met elsewhere, perhaps in supervision or in a support group.

Silences

The counsellor also uses silences constructively and does not get embarrassed by them, filling them with questions or her own experiences. The client can use the silence to reflect, think, get in touch with her deeper feelings, express her feelings.

Qualities

There are three qualities a counsellor uses as well as the basic techniques of active listening, reflection and questioning. These are empathy, acceptance and sincerity. Empathy is different to sympathy which inappropriately imposes the counsellor onto the client. Empathy means understanding the client's perception of the world and conveying this understanding deeply to the client. When a client feels this happening in the counselling relationship he or she can be released as though from a prison of isolation and fear – 'you really do understand what I feel'.

Acceptance means being able to suspend judgement and criticism and having what Carl Rogers, the founding father of counselling, called 'unconditional positive regard' for the client. In our society such an attitude contrasts starkly with the judgements and criticisms most of us receive and give for much of the time. Hence the need for long and intensive training for counsellors to become capable of suspending judgements and truly accepting of their clients. The biblical phrase 'loving the sinner but not the sin' describes the phenomenon well. Sincerity is the ability to be open, real, genuine and consistent with the client. The client must feel the counsellor is a real person, not just a professional doing a job.

Pitfalls

We have looked at the key skills and qualities used in counselling relationships and will now return to, and expand on, some of the main pitfalls for the warden who wishes to use counselling techniques at work.

Being too busy to listen – if you know you are genuinely too busy to listen then say so and negotiate a mutually convenient time to return – using assertive techniques if appropriate.

Asking too many questions, with emphasis on finding out facts – We can unintentionally impose our own need for certainty onto the client through a search for facts and meaning. We must suspend this need and allow the client to tell the story in her way accepting her emphasis on what is important for her. Constant questions will turn the counselling into an intellectual exercise shifting the focus away from feelings. The client will think that the details of the incident are more important to you than how she feels about it.

Rushing to provide practical solutions – to a presenting problem which may, in fact, only be the surface trivial concern of the client. Counselling is not about advice giving or solution finding. Untrained 'counsellors' may feel anxious and wish to make *themselves* more comfortable and competent by providing a quick practical solution hence:

Blocking the client's emotions – Most of us have difficulty in coping with at least one of our basic emotions (fear, grief, anger) and because of this find it too painful or uncomfortable to see these emotions expressed in others. In training, wouldbe counsellors have to acknowledge, explore and work on their own emotions in order that their own 'blocks' do not inhibit their responsiveness to clients.

Wanting to do everything for the client – As all wardens discover this ends up with inappropriate dependency by the client and does the client a lot of damage by taking away their opportunity for self-determination and increased self-esteem. This motive for wanting to do too much may stem from:

Wanting to be liked by the client – This may in turn originate from fear of not being liked, of needing approval from others in order to have a feeling of self-worth. The material on self-esteem, socialisation and rights in the section on assertiveness is very relevant here.

Identifying with the client – can be very tempting but is to be avoided. Once again we can unwittingly be more concerned with making ourselves feel better when we identify with a client's experience than with focusing appropriately on the client and his or her distress. In conversations between friends and colleagues identification and the sharing of problems can be mutually comforting – in counselling we must never forget who is the client.

Being threatened by culture/generation/class gap – We can feel insecure about the apparent differences between us and react defensively. Drawing on the key counselling skills and recalling our assertive rights can help counteract this tendency – we are all human beings with common needs and common rights.

Imposing our own values – We need to suspend our judgements and criticisms – they are not important – the client is the focus.

Not being able to cope with silence – We have found that many wardens have admitted to feeling uncomfortable with silences between them and their tenants but have learned through the listening exercises and other role plays in class the support and value of them when being the client. Once again we can fill the silence because of concern with our own needs not those of the client.

Show own anxiety to client – making client even more anxious. If you feel out of your depth say so and gently suggest referral to a more experienced counsellor.

Offering unsolicited insights and interpretations – Contrary to popular mythology this is only a tiny part of counselling and done inappropriately or too quickly makes the client feel resentful or threatened. Often the 'insights' can be given to make the 'counsellor' feel superior.

Betrayal of confidentiality – Counselling techniques can be very powerful and encourage clients to divulge a great deal about themselves and their private thoughts. There must be an explicit agreed contract of confidentiality or the implicit trust could be abused.

Going too deep – Clients need their defences and counselling techniques can be used manipulatively to break down people's defences for the gratification of the 'counsellor'. Virginia Woolf commented on 'the peculiar repulsiveness of those who dabble their fingers self approvingly in the stuff of others' souls'. Be very, very careful not to use counselling techniques to make yourself feel powerful, clever, skilful, important. Older people tend to feel powerless as it is and counselling should not be done in such a way as to exacerbate this.

Opportunities for the use of counselling skills

The most obvious use of counselling skills is following a bereavement. Grieving is sometimes said to follow four stages. Initial shock, grief or anger or guilt, despair and lethargy, re-emergence and adjustment. The warden can help the client accept the reality and pain of the loss, and eventually adjust and invest in new relationships.

As well as following bereavement there are many more situations in the day-to-day life of a sheltered housing scheme which lend themselves to the appropriate use of counselling techniques. Loss is a key experience for all of us and when we get older we face loss more and more frequently. We may lose our health, our independence and our mobility. We lose significant friends and relatives. We lose our jobs and our status. We have lost our home in the move to sheltered housing. Loss elicits the feelings of sadness and grief often because a new loss restimulates old, perhaps buried feelings and memories of earlier, even childhood losses but these feelings may be unacknowledged and unexpressed. Counselling techniques can help these feelings to be discharged safely and constructively. The warden does not have to be resolutely cheerful and positive, effectively encouraging denial of distress in the tenants in her scheme – she can choose to utilise and develop the sincere acceptance and understanding of the tenants she works with and truly listen to what they have to tell her.

Assertiveness

The Four Behaviours

We have found that many wardens, like much of the rest of the population, have misunderstood assertiveness. Yet after some basic training and information on what it is and is not, they have made dramatic changes both in the way they feel about themselves and in the way they behave toward others. And this is the core of assertiveness – self-image and consequent behaviour.

Try 'brainstorming' on four separate sheets of paper these four types of behaviour: passive, aggressive, manipulative and assertive. Include verbal and non-verbal communication, voice tone and volume, typical statements.

Then compare your results to the following summary:

Table 4.1 The Four Behaviours

	Assertive	**Passive**	**Aggressive**	**Manipulative**
Expression of views feelings wishes	clearly and appropriately states wants, thoughts & feelings whilst respecting others' rights. Considers compromise Wants win/ win situation.	doesn't state wants, thoughts or feelings, hopes others will guess. Always over-compromising, wants lose/win situation.	rudely expresses wishes thoughts or feelings with no regard for others. Never compromises. Hell bent on winning, others losing.	expresses wishes thoughts & feelings covertly & gets needs met by making others feel guilty. Pretends to compromise but wants win/ lose situation.
Belief in rights of self and others	believes in right to be treated with respect as an equal human being.	believes others' rights, wishes etc. are more important than own; backs down, gives up/in.	believes own rights wishes etc. are superior and more important than others; attacks.	pretends others are equal or superior but in fact puts them down, scapegoats, blames, cajoles, uses sarcasm.
Verbal content	I feel, I'd like, I think, I prefer	I'm sorry, I should, I ought, I'm hopeless, Not important really, Maybe, I'm afraid	You should, You ought, You must, You can't	

Verbal structure/ speech pattern and	Brief, succinct, fluent, clear, sincere, honest, appropriate volume.	Rambling, waffles, hesitant, quiet	Fluent, fast, opinions expressed as facts. Interrupts, bulldozes, loud.	Confusing, red herrings, excuses, insincere flattery, patronises, hints, smarmy.
Body Language/ Non verbal communica-tion	Gentle direct gaze, upright posture	Avoids eye contact, slumps, nervous fiddling.	Glaring, pointing, standing over, thumping.	Avoids eye contact, excessive smiling

Did your brainstorming cover similar ground? What are your differences? Do these indicate some misunderstandings about assertiveness? Circle the discrepancies in your notes and come back to them later when you have read more of this chapter.

Self-esteem and socialisation

Assertiveness (i.e. the ability to communicate openly, directly and honestly) is inextricably linked to self-esteem and this in turn is linked to how we were brought up and the general culture in which we find ourselves.

As children we are often discouraged from believing we have equal rights with others – we are told that adults or our brothers or sisters are more important. We are accused of selfishness or boasting if we express our wishes or praise our successes. We are beset with 'You should, you ought' so become very reliant on the opinions and approval of others to feel OK about ourselves. We learn passive, aggressive or manipulative behaviour as a response to being treated non-assertively.

Our culture conditions many women into believing that their job is to care for others, to put others' needs first. Therefore, if we refuse to do something for somebody we accuse ourselves of being selfish and uncaring.

We have found that many female wardens have identified with this explanation of the origins of their non-assertive behaviour. Their isolation and their ambiguous role have exacerbated the female tendency to fail into the so called 'compassion trap'.

To become more assertive we need to begin by noticing and correcting our internal critical dialogue, taking positive steps to increase our self-esteem. Try this exercise: write down on a piece of paper, 1) at least five things you like about yourself beginning with the statement 'I like myself because . . .' 2) at least five things you are good at beginning with 'I am good at . . .' You may be tempted to abandon or do the reverse i.e. sabotage it by writing all the things you do not like about yourself. Notice this process of 'negative inner talk' and then deliberately counteract it with the positive statements about yourself. If you genuinely want to improve your self-esteem you will encourage yourself to do this exercise often and with increasing confidence. Look at your lists from time to time and say them aloud or share them with a trusted friend, partner or colleague. Avoid people who put you down or do not take you seriously.

Rights

Alongside working to improve your self-image as part of becoming more assertive we encourage increasing awareness of your own and other people's rights as human beings. This is often called the Assertive Bill of Rights. We have found that discussion of this apparently simple list of rights can be very empowering for wardens – it provides much food for thought so we suggest you read this through very slowly, saying each one aloud to yourself.

1. I have the right to ask for what I want (notice this is not the same as '*get* what I want').
2. I have the right to express my own feelings, opinions and values and to be listened to, taken seriously and treated with respect.
3. I have the right to make my own decisions and to set my own priorities, independent of any other roles I may have (e.g. as wife, husband, mother, father, daughter, son and warden).
4. I have the right to say 'no' without feeling guilty.
5. I have the right to decline responsibilities *for* other people's problems (though I may have responsibility *towards* others).
6. I have the right to make mistakes, to change my mind and to celebrate my successes.
7. I have the right to say 'I don't understand' and to ask for an explanation from professionals and others.
8. I have the right to choose when to and when not to assert myself.

If some of these rights are hard to believe in for yourself then trace the origins of these beliefs. Challenge them and move on!

Non verbal communication or 'body language'

We can assist or hinder our assertiveness through what we 'say' non-verbally. Eye contact, facial expression, body movements and posture and breathing can all give clues to an observer about your state of mind.

Try this exercise. In private or with a trusted partner sit slouched in a chair looking at the floor. Then sit upright gazing straight ahead. Notice how these different postures make you feel. Then combine them with a verbal statement such as 'I'd like you to stop making that noise' – the likelihood is that when slumped and in the passive position the request sounded feebler than when you were in the upright position. Next try the exercise standing up; first in a slouched passive way, then in an upright assertive posture.

Verbal structures and techniques for assertiveness

Be specific – The golden rule and essence of verbal assertiveness is 'decide what you want' and state it simply, clearly and specifically to the other person, preferably using 'I' rather than 'If, we, one, you'. This apparently simple guideline is easier said than done, however, if we have built up patterns of passive, aggressive or manipulative behaviour particularly in response to others' non-assertive behaviour. This is why the earlier work on self-image, rights and posture is vital to underpin the belief in and impact of the verbal techniques.

Repetition ('broken record') – If you have not received a satisfactory answer you can then choose to speak as if you were a broken record using calm repetition of your statement or request. Stick to the point, do not be put off by or respond to irrelevancies or argument from the other person. Repeat yourself over and over again until you are heard.

Fielding the response ('fogging') – shows that you have listened to the other person's point of view by putting one sentence starting with 'I understand that you . . .' or 'I can see that you . . .' before your broken record sentence.

An example of these techniques:

Specific	Warden: 'Mrs Roberts, I would like you to get your own prescription today'.

Mrs Roberts: 'Come on dear, you'll be passing the shops won't you'

Broken Record and fogging — Warden: 'Yes, I will be passing the shops but I would still like you to get your own prescription today'.

There are countless opportunities for wardens to practice these three basic techniques since they are continually being asked to do things outside their job description yet which makes them feel guilty when refused. If you can practice them in groups using role-play you will realise how hard most people find sticking to the point, how easy it is to be side-tracked, how important it is to decide what *you* want. Watch your body language, your voice tone and do not over-apologise, ramble or make excuses.

For further practice and discussion on these and other techniques, read Anne Dickson's classic book on assertiveness (Dickson, 1982) and/or go to an Assertion class. Your local college almost certainly offers short courses in Assertiveness training and they can change your life!

Coping with Violence and Aggression

Increasingly wardens are expected to be able to cope with tenants who are aggressive or even violent. Yet only rarely is training in this provided nor do wardens often ask for it. As with many potential risks in life we often take a 'head in the sand' approach and assume that 'awful things won't happen to me'. We believe that it is in fact a good idea to raise awareness of potentially dangerous situations and how we and others can often compromise our safety – 'forewarned is forearmed'.

The terms violence and aggression cover everything from verbal insults and shouting to threats, physical attack, and rape. We would include racist, sexist and ageist abuse in aggression since the key factor in deciding if we have been a victim of aggression is our feeling of upset or injury.

Causes

As wardens you may be aware of the causes of some of the aggressive and violent behaviour you have to deal with. Sometimes people suffering from a mental illness such as Alzheimers Disease may be unawarely aggressive. The tenant on the wrong medication or with too much alcohol or in acute physical pain may be aggressive. But a very common cause of aggression is frustration which emerges in out of control anger. The root of anger is blocked choice and occurs when we cannot do or have what we want; for example when we are kept waiting for hours by public transport, or by a relative, nurse, doctor, social worker or warden who doesn't show up. And this 'natural' anger is exaggerated if combined with any of the other causes mentioned above, e.g. alcohol.

Effects

What happens if you are faced with a violent or aggressive person? Most people feel fear or 'shut-down', panic or a sensation of being 'frozen on the spot'. Typical reactions in the body are sweating, increased pulse rate, churning stomach, panting, pupils dilating. After the threat or incident has passed our body returns to normal but we may feel odd, unreal, depressed, flat, or even guilty. Once again the isolation of wardens is harmful to their emotional health – most of us need to tell someone about a frightening experience but if there is no one to tell or only unsympathetic ears available then we are inclined to suppress or deny this need. A good support network of wardens can be invaluable after unpleasant instances especially if the basic qualities and skills of counselling are employed – ensuring that an individual's distress is not invalidated or dampened by inappropriate sharing or advice giving. The simple opportunity to let off steam is invaluable.

Strategies for Preventing, Reducing and Coping with Aggression

Spend ten minutes reflecting on how you use your common sense and experience to predict, and therefore prevent, potentially threatening situations. These are probably sensible strategies which you have taken for granted. Try sharing these 'tips' with a group of wardens and see what common points emerge. Perhaps these are or could be in your wardens' manual.

These strategies may include:

- avoid working outside alone whenever possible and ensuring your manager, partner etc., know of your movements;

- ensuring your building is safe and secure and assertively complaining when it is not;
- using a personal alarm;
- assertively ensuring you obtain a full history of new tenants and are given details of any previous violence;
- on arrival get to know new tenants and learn about their history, whether they abuse alcohol etc., what events in the past have triggered off violence;
- not assuming that your experience and kind nature makes you impervious to danger;
- assertively refusing to put yourself into a situation you believe will be dangerous.

The process of identifying and acknowledging the positive and sensible steps you already take to avoid or minimise potentially dangerous situations can in itself be empowering.

The next stage is to consider how we cope constructively with unavoidable threatening situations:

- knowing you have a right not to be threatened or attacked and assertively acting on this by giving clear specific messages to the attacker "Stop" or "I refuse to listen if you speak to me like that";
- walking away from an abusive tenant saying you will speak to them later when they are prepared to speak calmly, i.e. not lingering to try to make the tenant feel/ behave better;
- trusting your instinct and noticing verbal and non-verbal clues that someone is 'trouble' and therefore taking extra care in your communication with them, staying calm;
- use active listening and reflective statement techniques so the tenant feels listened to and understood;
- not provoking the tenant by entering into an argument or slanging match, or by unnecessarily delaying them or by patronising them or by touching them or by standing over them;
- learning about non-verbal communication with people from cultures other than your own;
- learning breakaway and escape tactics or 'bash and dash' techniques.

After the incident what should be done? Certainly we need to let off steam as already discussed. But just as important is to tell your management, in writing if they are unavailable or don't take you seriously on the phone. Violent incidents should always be monitored and support provided. Too many wardens' managers underestimate the potential for violent incidents in sheltered housing schemes, taking the view that the tenants are 'little old ladies' and expect wardens to cope with whatever happens. Agencies should be prepared to prosecute tenants for assault on their staff and to take seriously evidence that staff are at risk. A balance has to be struck between providing care for tenants and care for staff.

Groups

As well as learning to be effective in one-to-one communication, wardens can also benefit from developing their knowledge and skills in working with groups. They have the opportunity to participate in an impressive range of groups – from case conferences to wardens' meetings to tenants' reminiscence sessions. The purpose, methods and members of these different types of groups vary but there are some general tips and ideas, derived from sociological group work theories, that we believe are useful to wardens.

Why Have Groups?

They may be able to offer support to members, to share information with other wardens, to share ideas and opinions, to make decisions, to break down barriers, to reduce isolation. The group may have several purposes or only one. The group may be short-lived or run indefinitely, it may be set up by the warden or by others. However, the overriding value of groups, any group, for wardens is to counteract their feelings of isolation and need to feel they belong somewhere, referred to in chapter one. Over and over again, we have been struck by the relief, support and even joy that wardens experience when meeting and getting to know each other on our training courses.

The case conference is a group set up explicitly to enable participants to pool information, opinions and anxiety. They promote inter-disciplinary working, team-work, co-operation, commitment and shared decision making. They can identify, analyse and help to solve problems. Case conferences can help transcend barriers between professionals and carers. Frequent contact tends to increase liking and increased liking increases contact – in other words success breeds success in this area. And wardens can feel stronger having the weight and authority of the case conference behind them rather than feeling vulnerable in standing alone. Wardens should be invited to case conferences involving their residents or can initiate their own conferences, with management back up if necessary.

Setting up a Group

In setting up a group it is always advisable to ensure that participants share responsibility for setting the objectives of the group and the methods to achieve them. Many wardens' support groups have failed because members' objectives were not clarified at the outset and turned out to be in conflict with each other. Avoid objectives that are over-ambitious and unrealistic given the time available. Agree in advance the method of arriving at decisions – consensus, majority vote, or unanimous decision. Also decide in advance whether the group is closed (i.e. membership fixed, no new members) or open (new members can join or leave at any time); decide too who is eligible and not eligible to join.

Ensure there is a ground rule of mutual respect ensuring listening, valuing, validating of each person's contribution. Think about practicalities like timing, numbers (maximum and minimum), catering, room size.

Running the Group

Groups can be run autocratically, democratically or permissively. We favour the democratic style where proposals are made, discussed and either agreed to or rejected. Avoid 'over-chairing' or tyrannising a meeting through anxiety – conflict is not necessarily a bad feature of groups as will be mentioned below under theory.

Avoid patronising and underestimating participants and empower them by encouraging everyone to challenge jargon and muddled thinking.

The chairperson's or leader's role may be to introduce everyone, help clarify objectives and keep people to them, and to facilitate the group so people are *heard*. The chair can model to the group the ideal behaviour, i.e. active listening. Avoid just swapping information and problems – ensure decisions and plans of action are made.

Be assertive – don't just follow and be reactive – challenge, confront, innovate, create and be proactive where appropriate.

Theory

Some basic awareness of the inevitable features of groups can help you to understand group behaviour or group 'dynamics'.

Stages
Most groups go through four stages called forming, storming, norming and performing. During the forming stage members meet, check each other out, find out rules, purposes and boundaries to the group. During storming people may rebel, argue, compete, set up cliques, withdraw; it is a necessary though often uncomfortable phase. The next phase norming is characterised by cohesion, greater trust and support. Performing comes next in which members resolve problems, harmonise, nurture, energise and perform.

Inclusion, control, affection
Another useful way of understanding behaviour in groups is to consider the factors inclusion, control and affection. Inclusion is concerned with the questions 'Do I want to be here, why am I here?' 'Am I included and wanted by the leader, the other participants?' Feeling you are out of place, are an outsider due to real or imagined differences between you and the other participants inhibits your performance in a group. Control is about influence and whether you have any or dare to use it and still be included. Affection is about whether other members like or love you. These three issues are addressed by everyone participating in groups and in explicit or hidden ways. Awareness of these processes can help the group leader or facilitator be more tolerant and patient or behaviour that seems inappropriate.

Decision making
An alternative way of commenting on behaviour in groups is to consider its relation to decision making.

Group decision making is a process. An understanding of the behaviour patterns which make up this process will enable you to make more appropriate contributions to improving or maintaining the group's efficiency in making and implementing decisions.

Behaviour in the group can be viewed from the point of view of what its purpose or function seems to be. When a member says something, is she primarily trying to get the group task accomplished (task), or is she trying to improve or patch up some relationships among members (maintenance), or is she primarily meeting some personal need or goal without regard to the group's problems (self-oriented)?

Types of behaviour relevant to the group's fulfilment of its TASK are given below:

1. *Initiating* – proposing tasks or goals; defining problems; suggesting procedure; contributing ideas.
2. *Seeking information or opinions* – requesting facts; seeking relevant information about group concern; asking for opinions; seeking suggestions and ideas.
3. *Giving information or opinions* – offering facts; providing relevant information about group concern; stating opinions or belief about a matter before the group; giving suggestions and ideas.
4. *Clarifying and elaborating* – interpreting ideas or suggestions; clearing up confusion; defining terms; indicating alternatives and issues before the group.
5. *Summarising* – putting together related ideas, re-stating suggestions after the group has discussed them; offering a decision or conclusion for the group to accept or reject.
6. *Seeking decision* – testing for readiness to make decision; seeking decision-making procedure.
7. *Taking decisions* – stating group's feelings in terms of a group decision; invoking the decision-making procedure.

Types of behaviour relevant to the group's remaining in good working order, having a good climate for task work and good relationships which permit maximum use of member resources – i.e. GOOD MAINTENANCE are:

1. *Harmonising* – attempting to reconcile disagreements; reducing tensions; getting people to explore their differences.
2. *Gate keeping* – helping to keep communication channels open; facilitating participation of others; suggesting procedures which permit sharing remarks.
3. *Encouraging* – being friendly, warm, responsive, indicating by facial expression or remark acceptance of other contributions.
4. *Compromising* – modifying, in the interests of group cohesion or growth; yielding status in conflict situations.

5. *Standard setting* – expressing or suggesting standards for the group to attempt to achieve.
6. *Standard testing* – attempting to evaluate the quality of the decision-making process in the group; testing whether the group is satisfied with its procedure.
   (Every group needs both kinds of behaviour, and needs to work out an adequate balance of task and maintenance activities).

Types of behaviour which are not directed to helping the group work but which actually interferes with effective group functioning – i.e. *SELF ORIENTED* behaviour are:

1. *Dominating* – trying to assert authority or superiority in manipulating the group, or certain members of it.
2. *Aggressing and blocking* – attacking group members or group ideas and suggestions; stubbornness beyond 'reason'.
3. *Recognition or help seeking* – drawing attention to oneself in various ways; attempting to call forth sympathy response through expressions of insecurity, personal confusion; deprecating oneself beyond reasonable limits.
4. *Pairing up* – seeking out one or two supporters and forming a kind of emotional subgroup in which the members protect and support each other.
5. *Special interest pleading* – speaking for particular interest (e.g. 'engineers', 'personnel', 'management') as a cover for prejudice or stereotypes which best fit the individual's needs and desires.
6. *Withdrawing* – trying to remove the sources of uncomfortable feelings by psychologically leaving the group.

These kinds of self-oriented behaviour arise because the individual is faced with certain problems in the group, problems of *identity, own goals and needs* versus group goals and needs, *control* and *intimacy*. These undercurrents cannot be ignored. They should be recognised and attempts made to integrate these individual needs with the group's goals.

Reminiscence Work in Sheltered Housing

Most wardens reminisce with the residents in their schemes on an informal one-to-one basis – it seems a common sense and natural thing to do. In some sheltered housing schemes and in many residential care homes and hospitals more formally planned and structured reminiscence work takes place in the form of regular group sessions. Research has shown that even people in the advanced stages of senile dementia can benefit from this kind of work. In addition there is often a spin off benefit in improved functioning and communicating outside the group.

Training

Most wardens are advised to go on one of the short courses introducing reminiscence work prior to setting up their own sessions. (For example with the Age Exchange Reminiscence Centre – address at the end of the book.) This is in order to help them explore the skills and resources needed and to consider strategies and methods for running reminiscence groups.

Why Reminiscence?

Firstly though we need to reflect further on why reminiscence is considered to be so valuable these days. We believe the key importance of it is the valuing of another person's life through listening to it and accepting it. There are links here with what we have said about the value and essence of counselling. Through knowledge and understanding of the details of a person's background we are likely to deepen our respect and recognition of their own individuality. Again there are links with other aspects of this book notably the emphasis throughout on the need to promote choice, rights, dignity and independence.

Many older people in sheltered housing have few or no surviving relatives and may have infrequent opportunities to reminisce spontaneously with those people with whom they spent their early years. By introducing reminiscence sessions the wardens may enable residents to expose forgotten links and memories and to increase compassion and understanding.

Skills Used

Skills needed in reminiscence work are listening, attending, accepting, resourcefulness, planning. Your experience in running other social group activities will come in useful in terms of knowing how groups form and function and you may wish to draw on some of the theory in the previous section.

Planning

You will need to carefully plan the sessions in advance – and decide on their purpose, duration, and frequency. You are strongly advised not to run them single-handed if at all possible and also to limit the size of the group according to the number of people with dementia or other special needs. You may find an experienced reminiscence worker in your area or perhaps a local historian or librarian interested in local history or perhaps a social worker. Workers may not wish to be paid.

Methods

Reminiscence work is not all about talking; it can and does take the form of writing, cooking, eating, painting, singing, smelling, dancing, drama, playing music or games, handling photos and objects, visits. If you get stuck in your sessions and seem to be going over the same ground consider changing the dominant method of reminiscence.

Resources

Resources for reminiscence work are available everywhere. Your own residents can provide small items such as photos, clothes, recipes, ration books, ornaments etc. Neighbours, families, museums, libraries and other institutions may be able to find larger items such as mangles, kitchen equipment, children's games, furniture, shopping items and so on. Word-of-mouth requests as well as using the local newspaper and radio can all be extremely fruitful in producing a rich variety of objects for reminiscence.

Depth not Breadth

The most productive reminiscence sessions do not skim over several topics but go deeply into only one or two. One warden told us she was involved with a group that spent two hours discussing apple pie recipes! In your pre-planning sessions choose a range of topics and then brainstorm each one in as much detail as you can manage. Topics can include health care pre-1948, shopping, food, markets, clothes, the kitchen, work in the home, work outside the home, war experiences, school, childhood games . . . the list is endless. Care needs to be taken to ensure that each topic is meaningful to each member of the group – be careful of discrimination against elders whose earlier lives were not spent in this country for example.

Stress

Everyone talks about stress now, even children. Research, media interest and countless books on the subject have ensured this.

Stress has been defined in many ways reflecting the various theories of its causes and effects. We will define it as force or stimulation or pressure on a person sufficient to produce strain or disruption to normal stable functioning.

Many wardens in sheltered housing for the elderly have suffered from stress largely unnoticed by anyone including themselves. Yet as we saw in Chapter 1 there are many features of the warden's role and of their place in an organisation's hierarchy that intrinsically produce problems for the post-holder. This section of the chapter aims to help you to a) identify your own symptoms of stress and their effects on those around you, b) reflect on their causes and c) consider some remedies.

It is worth remembering that we all need some pressure in order to feel alive. Some wardens, like some retired people, suffer stress through the boredom of having nothing to do.

Symptoms

Symptoms of stress can be physical – headaches, insomnia, stomach ache or they can be emotional/mental manifesting in feelings of failure, depression, inability to make decisions, helplessness, irritability, dread, suppression of feelings, or they can show in your behaviour – apathy, inconsistency, irrationality, absenteeism, low morale. At its worst, stress leads to total exhaustion, collapse or breakdown – commonly called burnout. There are said to be stages we go through before we reach total burnout and each one has its warning signs for sufferers and those around them. The scale ranges from never saying no, not taking days off at the beginning to alcohol abuse, withdrawal and physical and/or mental illness at the end. In a survey of social workers the most common feature of burnout was feelings of lack of personal accomplishment followed by emotional exhaustion and loss of feeling towards clients (Gibson, 1989).

Causes

What causes stress? Again research on this for different occupational groups, ages, personality types fills libraries everywhere. There are many ways of analysing and categorising the causes of stress but it is important to remember that individuals respond differently to the same external pressures. Our response to stress is always a personal and individual one. As Cooper, one of the country's leading researchers on stress, puts it 'Personality, coping strategies, the number and nature of life events, age, gender, ethnic background, social support' all contribute to effect vulnerability to stress (Cooper, 1988).

A productive way of analysing the causes of stress is to consider the extent to which the stress source is rooted in you as an individual, the people around you, the organisation, the community or the culture in which you live and work.

Individual – your own beliefs, attitudes and behaviour cause you stress. Wardens are often untrained for the demanding job they do and often blame themselves for the difficulties they encounter. Many are middle aged women lacking educational qualifications who have not been encouraged to believe in themselves, their skills and personal qualities. So often wardens are unassertive, never say no, work round the clock, and are full of self-blame and self-doubt.

Interpersonal – Others' expectations are high or contradictory. Wardens are not held in high regard by many tenants, relatives, managers, other professionals and this feeling of being taken for granted and general lack of respect is hurtful and stressful. Wardens are invariably excluded from teams and hence do not get involved in shared decision making. The feeling of exclusion is also isolating, hurtful and stressful. Wardens miss out on the formal and informal communication systems between people at all levels in their organisations.

Organisational – As we have already commented, wardens are a peculiarly ignored occupational group. They are expected to work effectively without regular or quality supervision or support from their managers and also to cope unaided with a job description intrinsically full of potential for role ambiguity and role conflict. Cooper states 'stress indicators found to relate to role ambiguity are depressed mood, lowered self-esteem, life dissatisfaction, low motivation to work and intention to leave'. Similarly 'role conflict leads to cardio-vascular ill health'. We see an interesting parallel between Cooper's demonstration of role conflict in dentists (where there was a clash between the idealised 'caring/healing' role and the reality of being an inflictor of pain) and in wardens (where there is conflict between the desire to care and the goal of promoting independence i.e. when real caring can be doing nothing for a tenant).

Returning to the issue of inadequate management support for wardens it is revealing that in the survey of social workers and stress referred to earlier, respondents ranked more support, appreciation and understanding from management as a way of ameliorating stress almost as highly as increased resources. Yet all too often wardens have told us that there is a 'wimp' culture prevailing which dictates that a worker would be made to feel inadequate for asking for help and support – 'if you can't stand the heat, get out of the kitchen'.

A further problem connected to wardens' isolation within the organisation is the lack of involvement in policy and decision making. This manifests itself nowhere more clearly than over allocations. Wardens say they feel powerless and totally lacking in influence over new care-in-the-community-inspired policies to place people say with a mental illness into their schemes. This is compounded by the wardens' and the organisations' lack of influence over the resourcing of community care. We looked at the impact of the community care changes on wardens and at how wardens can make an impact on the changes in Chapter 3.

The Community – The immediate environment of the sheltered housing scheme or estate may be a source of stress through high rates of vandalism and crime, noise, lack of sense of community.

Cultural – Stereotyping and prejudice about race, gender, age, sexuality and disability can affect wardens. They may have to tackle prejudice between residents or bias against themselves, often ending up feeling they cannot win whatever they do. Many employers have quite properly initiated equal opportunities policies throughout the organisation but wardens may once again feel too isolated and unsupported to implement them properly.

Interesting studies have been carried out comparing the extent of social support offered in different countries and the connection between this factor and physical health. It is apparent that the listening and acceptance offered by a partner, relative or close friend relieve stress and prevent ill health.

Other factors contributing to stress for wardens include shift work, long hours and living 'on the job' – the goldfish bowl syndrome described in Chapter 1. Also jobs entailing responsibility for people are now well recognised to be far more stressful than jobs with responsibility for things such as budgets, equipment and buildings. In fact wardens have responsibility for all these things and people too.

Common life events such as bereavement, divorce, having a baby, moving home, children leaving home all cause us stress and often trigger off physical illness.

Management of Stress

If you have managed to read all the previous pages without giving up, the chances are you are feeling stressed as a result! Seeing all these analyses of the causes of stress may be overwhelming at first but is a necessary process to go through before we can look constructively at some solutions and ways of coping with them.

A good starting point is to make a diagram listing the causes of stress in your life, perhaps using the framework described in the previous section, and the resulting symptoms.

Consider the ways that you already use to deal with these causes (include good and bad solutions).

Now reflect on the following suggestions to see if they can be added to your repertoire:

1 Relaxation and rest in which you plan and do take time out for yourself. This can range from luxuriating in a long hot bath to attending relaxation, yoga or meditation classes at your local college.
2 Assertiveness – from believing in your rights to saying no to inappropriate requests – see section earlier in this chapter and consider attending assertiveness training classes.
3 Enhance self-esteem, through assertiveness or any other method you can think of. Value your skills.
4 Take up hobbies that stimulate you physically and/or mentally.
5 Seek out friends/relatives to let off steam, express feelings safely.
6 Time management – see section on this in Chapter 6.
7 Set up a support group (see section on groups in this chapter).

8 Combine with others to challenge and change working practices that dis-empower, confuse or isolate you, perhaps via a trade union or the National Wardens Association.
9 Analyse a problem creatively and devise an action plan to deal with it.
10 Consider counselling, co-counselling (see Evison, 1983), or therapy for deep-rooted and long standing personal difficulties – they are not just for those who are ill but for anyone who wants to change.
11 Do anything constructive to tackle the feelings and the reality of powerlessness and helplessness – don't suffer in silence – you have a right to your feelings and you have a right to ask for support or change.

Report Writing

Most wardens have come on our course dreading the emphasis we place on learning report writing skills. If you are tempted to skip this section perhaps you share their resistance too. However, by the end of the course and a great deal of practice in report writing via the assignments, students tell us they are delighted with their achievement, their new found skill.

Unfamiliar to Wardens

At the beginning of the course some wardens say to us that they never write reports in their work. We reply that perhaps it is because no one, including themselves, thinks they are capable. Housing managers and professionals from other agencies such as Social Service Departments undervalue and even ignore the contribution to assessments that wardens can make if asked. Wardens are left off circulation lists, not invited to case conferences, not asked to provide information or contribute their views. Wardens resent this and tell anyone who is prepared to listen that they know the tenants in their scheme for example, that their relationship has been developed over a number of years and that the warden has an extensive knowledge of each tenant's circumstances. Another instance of wardens not writing things down is when they wish to make referrals to other agencies. Invariably requests are made over the phone and this is often quite appropriate. However, more complex referrals or those verbal ones that appear to have been ignored lend themselves perfectly to some form of written communication, a memo or perhaps even a report.

Reports are necessary

Some students expect we will ask them to write essays but we never do. The NWCC is, quite rightly in our view, intended to be a practical, vocational and skills-related course. In your paid work you will never be asked to write essays, nor are you likely to be filled with an urge to volunteer them. But the reverse is true of reports as we have explained above. Most of you work for large, complex organisations, typically structured in a hierarchy or bureaucracy, like a family tree. In small organisations or even families verbal communication may be all that is needed. When large numbers of people are employed, verbal communication is likely to be inadequate and the circulation of reports or memos can: save time; ensure clarity, understanding and accountability; keep people up-to-date.

Value to wardens

One outcome of our emphasis on report writing has been that wardens know how to read reports as well as write them. Due to unfamiliarity wardens can be intimidated by reports reinforcing the familiar feeling of exclusion and isolation. Wardens can feel and be more involved in the work of the whole organisation through the 'knock on' effects of learning about report writing. Qualified wardens have told us that they no longer file incoming reports away 'to look at one day' but read them critically and with greater understanding of their purpose than before.

Do's and Don'ts

So what is the purpose of a report, what should one contain, how should it be set out? The answers to these questions come alive if you look at an actual report produced by your organisation. Ask your manager for a recent internal report (*not* the Annual Report or accounts) if you don't have one in your office.

Write down the answers to these questions:

1 For whom is the report intended?
2 Who wrote the report?

3. What is the purpose of it?
4. What is the subject of it?
5. Does it assume existing knowledge?
6. Is the report for information, decision or action?
7. Study how the report is divided up – usually by numbered headings or paragraphs, sometimes with subsidiary paragraphs. Note down briefly the areas covered within each main numbered section or paragraph. If each one has a heading that is all you need.
8. At the end of the report is there a Summary, Conclusions, Recommendations? What is the reader asked to do?

The answers to these questions begin to show some of the 'do's' and 'don'ts' of report writing. A report is *always* structured in order to clearly separate points and help the reader. Imagine giving a friend your shopping list – if everything is jumbled up she will find it much harder and more time consuming than if you had made separate mini-lists of things you needed from each shop.

A report needs to begin with a title (for ease of filing and retrieval), a date, a statement of who wrote it and who it is for, an indication of its purpose and subject, perhaps a summary.

For example:

REPORT ON:	*MRS A. JONES, Flat 1, Acacia House, Acacia Avenue, NW6,*
FROM:	*Angela Brown, Sheltered Housing Warden, Acacia House, Acacia Avenue, NW6*
TO:	*Team Leader, Social Service, Area 1*
DATE:	

The report must be clear, comprehensible (avoid jargon), complete, and specific; it should avoid being vague, waffly, incomplete, over long. The structure will vary according to the purpose of the report but usually the framework is an introduction or background, findings, conclusions, recommendations. Each of these headings is numbered and then sub-divided with further numbers.

(See Chapter 6 for discussion on record keeping and access to records).

Try to make each subheading or paragraph distinct from the rest without overlap – getting the headings clear is a most important part of report writing. Make your sentences and paragraphs relatively short. Sentences should ideally not exceed 25 words and paragraphs of more than 20 lines are off-putting to some readers.

Figure 4.1 SAMPLE REPORT FORMAT AND NUMBERING

DATE TITLE TO FROM

SUMMARY (OPTIONAL)

1. INTRODUCTION

2. FINDINGS

    2.1

    2.2

    2.3 ETC.

3. CONCLUSIONS

    3.1

    3.2

    3.3 ETC

4. RECOMMENDATIONS

    4.1

    4.2

    4.3 ETC

The conclusions are where the report writer gives her opinions, based on the facts described under findings. A common mistake for beginners to report writing is to introduce new material not referred to earlier.

The recommendations should state crisply what the writer wants done and by whom, again each point should have had a clear reference to it earlier.

References and Further Reading

Cooper C, Cooper R and Eaker L (1988) *Living with Stress* Harmondsworth: Penguin.
Dickson A (1982) *A Woman in Your Own Right, Assertiveness and you* London: Quartet Books Ltd.
Evison R and Horobin R (1983) *How to Change Yourself and your World* Sheffield: Co Counselling Phoenix.
Gibson F, McGrath A and Reid N (1989) *Measures of Stress in Social Work Today* 20 April 1986, pp. 16–17.
Halmos P (1978) *The Faith of the Counsellors* London: Constable.
Houston G (1984) *The Red Book of Groups* London: Rochester Foundation.
Institute of Housing and National Federation of Housing Associations (1990) *Tackling Violence against Housing Staff* London: National Federation of Housing Associations.
Kindred M (1984) *Once Upon a Group* 20 Dover Street, Southwell, Nottingham, NG25 0ED: Michael Kindred.
Lindenfield G (1986) *Assert Yourself, How to reprogramme your mind for positive action* Northamptonshire: Thorsons Publications Ltd.
Mc Derment L (1988) *Stress Care* Social Care Association.
More W (1990) *Aggression and Violence* Birmingham: PEPAR Publications.
Mulligan J (ed) (1988) *The Personal Management Handbook – How to make the most of your potential* London: Sphere Books Ltd (covers a variety of topics included in this chapter and more).
Norris A (1986) *Reminiscence* Bicester: Winslow Press.
Scrutton S (1989) *Counselling Older People, A Creative Response to Ageing* London: Edward Arnold.
Visal Hall J (1988) *Report Writing* London: The Industrial Society.

CHAPTER 5
Working with an Ageing Community

Introduction

In this chapter we examine some key features associated with working with older people, notably ageism, rights and risks, advocacy and assessment. We also consider the particular needs of ethnic elders, especially the extra problems they may encounter as a result of discrimination, prejudice or simply a lack of understanding of their specific needs. Finally, we consider the wardens' role as advocate in ensuring their tenants receive the level of services due to them from the NHS, together with discussing the currently topical issue of drugs and medication for older people and how far the warden's role should extend in this area.

An overall theme of the areas considered here is that of considering the effects of our own – and other people's – attitudes towards the elderly, together with the self-perception older people may have.

Wardens frequently face a set of conflicting demands – their job is to encourage the independence of older people, yet society presents the image of the elderly as a dependent and needy group who should be looked after by those paid to care for them. This chapter therefore explores aspects of this dilemma and considers how wardens can contribute by examining the skills, knowledge and understanding they need in order to do so.

Ageism

We love to pigeonhole people in our society. When meeting someone new we automatically seek to find out various facts about them – which combination of facts we are keen to have depends on the circumstances. They include name, age, whether married, number and ages and sexes of children, how long they have lived/worked somewhere and so on. Possession of this information makes us feel more comfortable and secure. Our unconscious fears and fantasies can be contained and managed if we can 'control' the other person through knowing who they are.

From the earliest possible age we learn that knowing a person's age is very important. Very young children are encouraged to share their ages with each other establishing an immediate pecking order from playschool upwards. The sense of superiority and inferiority thus derived stays with most people for life. The conception we form of old is always relative to our own age – at 5 everyone over 10 is old, at 50 everyone over 70 is old, at 80 people over 90 seem old.

Once we have learned a person's age we then make assumptions about them and these are often ageist, i.e. based on stereotyping and prejudice.

Low Expectations

We may have low expectations of older people or they may have them of themselves. As the Prince of Wales stated 'Older people act out the role which society has cast on them' quoting evidence of low participation in all kinds of activities once retirement is reached (The Guardian 16.5.90). Immobility and lack of money are not the only reasons why older people don't go out – there can be a decline of energy and weakening of will 'I'm getting on a bit, I don't think I'll bother' and the world shrinks though lack of use. The media and wellmeaning paid or unpaid carers contribute towards this process. Journalist Katharine Whitehorn commented 20 years ago on 'our deadly kindness in expecting (them) to take it easy, slacken off, stop trying; we turn (old people) into bits of old driftwood in the chimney corner and then dislike (them)' (Whitehorn, *Observer* 9.12.73).

Has there been much change in 20 years? Do we accept and expect contributions to help?

High Expectations

Recently there has been a tendency to swing the other way regarding the potential of old people to care for themselves and do fantastic things until great old age. We read accounts of 95-year-olds delivering meals on wheels, elderly politicians and of writers and keep fit instructors in their 70s and 80s. This can be very oppressive for those older people who have neither the ability or the inclination to excel in later life. And there is something ageist in the focus on these expectations as they are held up as examples of how we can still behave as though we are young. It seems that to be old and unfit and unachieving is being implicitly criticised through the emphasis on these capable others. This refusal to accept and even celebrate normal ageing nowhere manifests itself more clearly than over appearance – most of us, especially women, from age 20 to 100 are delighted when told 'you don't look your age'. We are led to believe by society and the media that to look old is undesirable and we spend vast amounts of money in trying to stay young looking. One enlightened actress when being photographed said 'Don't retouch my wrinkles – it took me so long to earn them'. A revolution will have occurred when 'you look your age' is a compliment.

Language

One of the most habitual and deeply ingrained aspects of our prejudices manifests itself in our language. Implicit sexism in our speech for example will take many years to eradicate. Similarly our language in regard to older people is often thoughtless at best and abusive at worst. 'Old folk, geriatrics, wrinklies, little old lady' are all offensive. Even the term 'the elderly' is now being questioned and at least one London Borough now insists on its replacement by the phrase 'older people'.

Myths and Professional Attitudes

Further incorrect assumptions about old age are that ill health is inevitable and that memory and capacity to learn decline inexorably. See the section on An Ageing Population in Chapter 3 for some figures that contradict these myths.

This generalising about old age is perhaps the worst aspect of ageism, this assumption that all old people are the same. 'People are people at 19 or 90 and are just as conscious of their own individual identity' as Mary Stott said 20 years ago in a pioneering article on the dangers of age stereotyping (Stott, *The Guardian* 22.11.73). This stereotyping is especially unforgivable in professional attitudes notably in medicine and social work. Wardens have told us over and over again of the condemnations and dismissive attitudes and practices of professionals they deal with. Alison Norman in her booklet on Ageism summarises the ageism of GPs neatly:

> poor communications, automatic attribution of ill-health to old age, reluctance to refer older people for investigation, inappropriate

> repeat prescriptions, over willingness to sedate, failure to recognise dementia and depression, lack of cooperation with social services departments.
>
> (Norman, 1987)

Scandal after scandal has been reported in the media of the ill treatment of older people in long-stay geriatric wards. In one recent case it was reported that nurses demonstrated lethargy and lack of interest towards their elderly patients, playing cards while catheter bags over flowed. Nurse Graham Pink has achieved considerable notoriety during 1990/91 for his whistle-blowing activities in drawing attention to the low levels of staffing assigned to geriatric wards.

Two press reports in 1990 commented on older women being excluded from routine cervical smear tests and how few clinical trials are carried out on people over 65, cancer being especially poorly treated (*The Guardian* 12.1.90, 27.4.90). We considered in Chapter 3 the low priority social workers have given to working with older people. Many writers suggest that the poor quality care offered to older people by professionals stems from a denial of the carer's own fears of ageing, dying and death. The body is cared for but the emotions are neglected. The hospice movement dramatically challenges this pattern and its enlightening and inspiringly positive approach to care of the dying is slowly filtering into ordinary hospitals.

Carers, paid and unpaid, of elderly people have low status and this effects the way they perceive themselves and their work. One of the most positive outcomes of our course is the greater value placed by our students on their work with the elderly.

Professionals have been guilty in the past of patronising older people with a 'we know best' attitude – the new concept of empowerment of clients has been slow in filtering through to this client group. But now in residential and community care greater efforts are being made to secure the wishes of the client or customer in every area from desired bed time to views on health care policy. Consultation is a crucial aspect of the new community care changes (see Chapter 3).

The connection between ageist attitudes and lack of acceptance of risk in older people is explored in the next section.

Retirement

Aspects of ageism that we have not touched on so far are age-related retirement and recruitment policies. We are a long way behind the USA and most European countries in terms of legislation banning these blatantly discriminatory practices. The potential of many 50-, 60-, 70- and 80-year olds to contribute productivity to the economy is wastefully and shamefully prevented by these tyrannical and obsolete practices. Some writers have even called for legislation banning all information about a persons age combined with law making it illegal to exclude anyone from a job because of age.

A related aspect of ageism to consider is the assumption that poverty is inevitable in old age. Many academics have criticised the taken for granted assumption that we will be poor when we are old. Perhaps in 10 or 20 years time Britain will see a united political movement run by and for older people on the same lines as the Gray Panthers in the USA.

Rights and Risks

Wardens are often attracted to work in sheltered housing by its philosophy of promoting independent living for older people. They believe everyone, including older people, has a right to live without unnecessary restrictions or indignities. Many wardens have worked in residential or hospital care prior to becoming wardens and disliked the regimes, lack of choices and passivity they observed. However, sheltered housing as a concept was rather short-sighted as explored in Chapter 1. Previously independent, able-bodied residents age and can become physically or mentally frail. They may develop senile dementia and cause great concern to those around them by their neglect of themselves or by their actions being dangerous to others, e.g. leaving gas taps on unlit. The original intention of the sheltered housing pioneers was that such people would automatically be moved on to residential accommodation. But times and policies have changed – there is now a greater emphasis on helping people remain 'in the community', on preventing admission to residential care and on promoting 'normalisation' i.e. people's rights to lead as near normal life as possible. A greater range of domiciliary and day care services are available to enable this. However, wardens often feel that they bear the brunt of such 'care in the community' policies, that the risks and danger their residents place themselves and others in are not acceptable, and that the support services are not adequate in terms of quality or quantity to render these risks acceptable. People can confuse risk with challenging but safe behaviour;

good assessment and liaison can help all those involved to distinguish the two.

Ageism and Contradictions

The idea of 'acceptable risk' is often problematic for other tenants in a scheme or for neighbours or relatives. People are often ageist, paternalistic or illogical in their attitudes towards risk in older people. We have to let our children take risks the older they get as part of growing up and achieving independence – if we keep them in cotton wool they are unable to think or do things for themselves. As adults we knowingly take risks by smoking, driving too fast, not exercising enough, eating the wrong food, drinking too much, embarking on dangerous sports. Yet these activities are allowed or encouraged in the name of choice and freedom of the individual. Why cannot the same reasoning be applied to the old person who wishes to eat the wrong things, refuse hospital treatment, drink a bottle of gin a day? People say 'she can't be sane to do such things, we must look after her, we know what's best for her' – but our great grandchildren in the next century may look back on our reckless death accelerating habits (e.g. smoking) and assume we too were 'mad' and ought to have been locked up. Society is hypocritical about risk taking and wardens need to reflect on the risks they personally take in their own lives, apparently sanely, to help them to be less judgemental of the risk taking by their tenants.

Choice

Human beings need to make choices even if they are illogical or not sensible. Anger is the outcome of blocked choice and is often turned inwards in the form of depression. Older people losing their physical or mental abilities understandably resent this process and restriction to their lives. Admission to residential care can compound the sense of helplessness and lack of choice and apathy and depression result. The apparently cantankerous and obstructive behaviour by a person fiercely resisting all well meant offers of help may be evidence of a healthy and life preserving spirit which should be respected and even celebrated.

Independence

Wardens often go into sheltered housing work as they are kind and caring people. This desire to help can be in conflict with the need to keep people independent, promote rehabilitation and tolerate risks. To refuse to get a prescription or make a cup of tea on the grounds that the resident will do themselves more good by doing it themselves tends to make wardens feel guilty, uncaring and neglectful. We all like to be dependent and to be looked after at times and knowing when to respond and when not to respond to these needs is part of the complex job of being a warden.

Relatives, other tenants and the media can exacerbate this 'safety first' approach. Wardens, through their isolation, are especially prone to anxiety about implementing a 'hands-off', risk-taking approach. Wardens worry about their professional image and reputation and can find it hard to explain to others that what they see as neglect is part of a positive policy of caring. Wardens must seek and get the full support of their managers in such cases.

The Community

Wardens are also in a particularly invidious position by having to balance the rights of one resident against the rights of all the others in the scheme. Social workers can be particularly insensitive to the stress wardens experience in living on site with the possibility of regular and often angry complaints of other residents. Sheltered housing schemes are communities and the relationships between the warden and each tenant should not be ignored. Wardens can practice assertively explaining this to other agencies and professionals. Community care is often dogged by the NIMBY problem – i.e. it's a good idea but 'Not In My Back Yard'. Wardens can be helped to carry the stress of having people with dementia in their schemes by being part of a team. Wardens should feel supported, valued and involved by a multi-disciplinary team and if they are not they could practice assertively asking why not?

Such teams can pool their detailed knowledge of a situation and keep the assessment process alive and productive. They can also work creatively at risk reduction and management. For example cookers can be disconnected or removed, gas fires replaced with convector heaters, electric kettles introduced, reality-orientation techniques utilised, respite care offered. There is a wide variety of resources for assistance with the management of risk and wardens should not expect themselves or be expected by others to be experts on this. The social services department's principal officer for the elderly, the psychogeriatrician, the local Alzheimers Disease Society, the National Carers Association may all be able to offer specialist advice as well as the usual GP and social worker sources.

Loss

We mentioned earlier that the original intention of sheltered housing was that people becoming physically or mentally frail would be moved into residential accommodation. As stated community care policies have reduced this practice as well as greater awareness that often more harm than good can result from such a move. The loss of a home with its familiar smells, sights, and people can lead to real grief. If combined with replacement by institutional care the outcome may be despair, apathy and accelerated death. A mentally confused person may function better at home in familiar surroundings than in a residential home or hospital. The person may become more confused and may fall or wander more than before. Admission to hospital does not prevent falls, contrary to the expectations of many relatives. The job of the warden is to alert relatives to the possibilities of more harm than good arising from a move and to educate them about the balance between rights and risks.

Advocacy and Empowerment

Wardens are ideally placed to be advocates for tenants and/or to help empower them. Advocacy is a system whereby a trusted friend/neighbour/volunteer/worker accompanies the user of a service to a meeting with say a doctor or social worker. The advocate keeps a focus throughout on the user and their expressed needs, echoing these if unheard to the professionals. The advocate acts as a support, a go-between or an intermediary for the user or client. The advocate can also assist with phone calls and letters but has to ensure that they are not working in such a way as to disempower the client. Empowerment is another currently topical concept, relevant to wardens in that it can help to address ageism. Older people can be oppressed by both the benevolent or the malevolent actions of others. Instead they need to have their wishes sought out and respected and to be involved in a meaningful way in planning processes. Wardens can work individually and collectively to highlight the potential for advocacy and empowerment in their work and show the other agencies and professionals that these concepts should not and need not be restricted to work with people with learning difficulties or mental health problems.

For example, older people living in sheltered housing may turn to the warden for help with making a complaint about a service. We believe that taking on or indeed seeking out this role is a vitally important aspect of a warden's job. The fact that it does not appear in the job description may be simply another example of the undervaluing of the reality and potential of the work.

The NHS and Community Care Act 1990 requires local authorities to take account of the needs and wishes of clients and to establish complaints procedures (see Chapter 3).

Wardens can utilise their assertive and report writing skills to advantage when acting as advocate for their tenants. Arguments need to be put over in a determined manner but avoiding abuse, and should always be put in writing. If the phone is used follow it up with a letter confirming the contents of the call.

Assessment

Wardens' potential for careful assessment of the social and housing needs of residents is undervalued by their own organisations, by relatives and by SSDs. Indeed one of the reasons we teach report writing skills on the NWCC is to enable wardens to contribute more effectively to the assessment process from which they are all too often excluded.

New Emphasis in Law on Assessment

Properly organised and broadly based assessment of an individual's needs is a key aspect of the 'Griffiths' changes in community care which are explained in detail in Chapter 3. For people 'whose needs extend beyond health care or whose needs for social care would not benefit by simple advice' SSDs will, from April 1993, be responsible for arranging assessments for people applying for domiciliary, day or residential care. The White Paper preceding the legislation implementing the main thrust of Griffiths' recommendations states that 'all agencies and professions involved with the individual and his or her problems should be brought into the assessment procedure where necessary'. Housing officers are included in the long list of such professionals.

Assessment for appropriate housing is also referred to in the White Paper: 'housing needs should form part of the assessment of care needs' and 'Social Services Authorities will need to work closely with housing authorities, housing associations in developing plans for a full and flexible range of housing'. The 1992 joint Housing and Social Services circular referred to in Chapter 3 reinforces this emphasis on the need for collaboration between the two agencies.

Wardens' Expertise

We believe that wardens are ideally placed to share their observations with other professionals. They usually have an awareness of how each resident functions on a day-to-day basis, of the range and extent of social support available to and used by, the resident, of a sudden or gradual change in functioning, health or happiness. Wardens build up an expert knowledge about practical ways people are helped or hindered by the housing, medical and social services and they can, and should in our view, be encouraged to contribute this wisdom at case and operational levels. As we can see in Chapter 6, Anchor Housing have already redefined their wardens' role in the light of the care in the community legislation, clearly stating that they are to be the key worker in identifying the care needs of their residents and in acting as care manager once a care plan is in place. It is to be hoped that other wardens' employers consider a similarly clear approach in recognising the contribution wardens can make.

Guidelines

We have found that not only do wardens lack training and encouragement to put their assessments in writing but also the 'know how' of professional assessments i.e. the jargon, the format, the scope. The rest of this section will cover the range of issues to be considered by wardens making assessments.

1. *Remember the resident's wishes* – This seems blindingly obvious but in pressured, dramatic or dangerous situations the wishes of the resident can be forgotten. Relatives, GPs, social workers or wardens may be so anxious, angry, preoccupied or busy that their own needs and wishes are dominant and no one remembers to voice the wishes of the old person concerned. Often wardens can act as an advocate for the old person – an appropriate aspect of their role in our view.

Elderly people are often referred for help by others who have not first checked that help is wanted or needed.

2. *Beware of residents 'underasking' for help* – Many elderly people feel ashamed or afraid to ask for help and wardens can use counselling qualities and techniques to notice and acknowledge these feelings. Wardens can also gently challenge their residents' own ageism if they seem prepared to 'suffer in silence'.
   Ensure that a resident's emotional problems are identified as well as practical needs. People are often not aware of the full range of services available or are misinformed so may not ask for a certain facility. Wardens can pass on their own firsthand knowledge of the local day centres, residential homes etc and can rectify ignorance and misunderstandings.
3. *Ensure the carer's wishes and needs are taken into account* – The 1986 Disabled Persons Act lays a duty on local authorities to consider the capacity of carers to go on caring. Assessments are incomplete if they exclude reference to, and involvement of, the main carers. The full 'care network' should be identified.
4. *Assessment should not be rushed* – assessors need to be patient and sensitive before full understanding is reached. Hence wardens are in a prime position to enhance other people's 'one off' assessments of their resident, as they can add observations made over the preceding days or weeks – most wardens are required to have daily contact with residents and it is quite extraordinary that this is not capitalised on more by other professionals.
5. *Take account of, and attempt to reduce, communication difficulties* – These may be due to sensory impairment (blindness or deafness), language, jargon or illness. With people who are blind or deaf you may need to educate others about the 'does he take sugar' attitude so common amongst the public, even professionals who should know better. Model good practice through your own behaviour. For residents who do not speak English ensure an interpreter is on hand when the social worker, GP or home care organiser visit but be sensitive to situations where an overbearing close relative does not make the best translator. Jargon is a barrier to understanding and is used unthinkingly by almost all professionals. 'Part III', 'voids', 'mentally frail', 'criteria', 'eligibility', '2.5', 'networks', are examples of words that can be used in assessments,

meaning nothing to the old person or their carer who through embarrassment may not admit to this. Illness can confuse or depress anyone and especially older people who may be particularly prone to feeling vulnerable, powerless and dependent. They may agree to suggestions regarding their future care that, when feeling well again, they subsequently regret.

6. *Ensure clear thinking about risk* – (see preceding section on rights and risks).
7. *Ensure that a full multi-disciplinary assessment is made if you think it is necessary* – The other agencies and professionals can and must work together despite their lack of resources and professional and bureaucratic barriers. The Audit Commission Report on Community Care 1986 stated that successful community care included 'a focus on action, not on bureaucratic machinery; locally integrated services, cutting across agency boundaries; a multi-disciplinary team approach'. In view of the current low priority given to work with older people in many SSDs the initiative for setting up psychogeriatric assessments or case conferences or network meetings may be taken quite appropriately by wardens. If you want more involvement from other professionals than is forthcoming, be assertive, use the broken record technique, write it down!
8. *Remember the resident has strengths too* – the focus of an assessment should not just be on disabilities or what the resident cannot do but also on their abilities and what they can do. Once again wardens are in a prime position for knowing and sharing an apparently frail, helpless and dependent old person's hidden talents and abilities.
9. *Record facts to back up your opinions* – Social workers and GPs tend to be rather dismissive or impatient with referrals that are full of the views and wishes of the referrer but without evidence to back them up. It is rather like accusing someone of guilt but putting forward no evidence or proof. Wardens could make their opinions carry more weight if they shared their specific, comprehensive and detailed observations of, say, behaviour over a period of time and then argued that for these reasons a certain course of action should follow. For example replace 'she wanders and is at risk' with 'on five occasions in the last two weeks she has left the building at 3 a.m. wearing only her underwear and has been found by the police in the middle of the motorway

on each occasion – I therefore think she is a considerable risk to herself and others and I request that . . .'

Working with Ethnic Elderly Groups

There is no doubt that members of ethnic groups growing old in this country face difficulties resulting from the ageing process and the discriminatory attitudes they may encounter – which they share with their indigenous counterparts. However, they may also have to cope with hostility and discrimination because of the colour of their skin, plus the fact that services are not easily accessible to them. This can also be compounded by the fact that large numbers of ethnic elderly people are concentrated in our inner city areas, and thus may be living in conditions of deprivation and possibly poverty.

Alison Norman (1986), in her influential study of the problems faced by elders from the ethnic minority communities examines these issues in depth and offers a number of ways in which action can be, and is being, taken to address them.

The Provision of Special Sheltered Schemes

In terms of the housing needs of this group the evidence points to the need for the provision of specialist sheltered housing schemes designed and managed around the needs of particular ethnic elderly groups.

This challenges the view that such provision is unnecessary, since in cultures other than our own, elders are looked after by their families. However, the extended family concept for families living in Britain is being eroded by pressures such as the economic and social structure, size of accommodation available and incompatible lifestyles.

Sheltered housing thus offers a refuge to vulnerable ethnic elderly people, in particular those who do not speak English and who have previously depended on families for support, since it offers a ready-made community of peers together with the support of a warden. The warden's role in these schemes is often extremely demanding; one warden of such a scheme who attended our course was in constant demand as an interpreter in addition to the other elements of the job. This particular warden also felt he had a responsibility to ensure that tenants remained outward looking and continued to participate in the life of the wider community, worshipping, visiting cafés and clubs as before. He perceived a tendency for his residents to expect the scheme to meet the whole range of social and cultural needs of its residents which, he felt, would not only result in a very closed community, but which would put tremendous pressure upon the warden to oversee and possibly even provide, the services himself, thus creating high levels of dependency.

The Need to Work with Ethnic Community Groups

Provision of specialist sheltered housing calls for close attention to the needs of the ethnic community being served, preferably at the planning state of any project. Community groups must be consulted; racial, religious and cultural needs must be fully understood from the outset in order to avoid problems of incompatibility at the allocations stage.

The National Federation of Housing Associations have produced *Race and Housing*, a guide for housing associations in this area; the working party report produced in 1984 by Age Concern England and Help the Aged Housing Trust, *Housing and related problems among elders in ethnic minorities* contains ideas for practice which continue to be relevant. In general, provision for ethnic elders tends to be generated by members of particular ethnic community groups working under the wing of a housing association having the development and financial expertise to support the project. Such grass-roots provision in general ensures that schemes are developed, let and managed with the specific needs of the ethnic groups in question firmly to the forefront.

Housing associations and local authorities which have few or no links with local ethnic community associations face greater difficulties in making contact with potential tenants from ethnic groups, and also face the problems of being seen as primarily 'white' organisations. This causes particular problems at the stage of allocations. All this is of course despite the best intentions and fully spelt-out equal opportunities policies of the organisations concerned.

This adds weight to the argument for the need to provide specialist sheltered housing which enables members of ethnic groups to stay within their own communities from which they can draw mutual support. Their past experiences may have included feelings of isolation, loneliness, fear of (or actual) racial harassment, and language difficulties, meaning that an offer of a place in a predominately white, or widely racially or culturally mixed sheltered housing scheme could be perceived as likely to continue, exacerbate or replicate such past experiences. Comfort and support can be drawn from being with their peers, and the warden, who will ideally be a member of the same ethnic group or with specialist knowledge and understanding of their needs, can encourage the growth of the community within the scheme whilst encouraging continued links with the wider community.

Specialist Sheltered Schemes – the Ghetto Argument

The view is sometimes expressed that, just as sheltered housing itself could be said to 'ghetto-ise' older people, the provision of schemes targetted towards specific groups intensifies this perception even further. This particular subject often causes much debate amongst students, who are keen to carry out their own research in order to test out this hypothesis. Our students at college, coming as they do from such a wide variety of organisations including many inner London Boroughs with a huge diversity of racial mix, find it rewarding to use each others' networks and contacts to visit different types of scheme and subsequently report and evaluate their findings.

The general conclusions seem to be that those schemes targetted towards a particular cultural or ethnic group seem to provide greater satisfaction for their tenants than schemes which previously housed indigenous older people and which in recent years have made an effort to offer vacancies to a wider racial mix. Often those ethnic elders housed in the latter type of scheme continue to feel isolated, perhaps being unable to communicate with other residents, and sometimes even with the warden. These findings bear out the countrywide research which has been carried out for the past ten years or more, and which is detailed by Norman (1985).

Discrimination – the Need to Understand and Challenge it

We have been discussing here an area of discrimination and prejudice against old people which some, but by no means all, wardens may find themselves in the position of challenging. Some wardens working in rural areas, or areas where there is little or no racial diversity, may consider this issue has nothing to do with them. However, we feel it is an important issue for all those working with older people to consider, for the reasons we outline below.

Firstly, we none of us live in a society which is free from social differences between groups and individuals. Indeed, a sheltered housing scheme could be seen as a microcosm of such a society. Whilst racial discrimination can be seen as one of the most prevalent and destructive examples of such differences, an understanding of this type of discrimination can help us to understand prejudice generally. This includes of course, ageist attitudes, together with prejudice based on gender, sexual orientation, disability, religious or cultural beliefs. As we know, wardens are in a key position to assertively challenge such discrimination and can better do so armed with knowledge and understanding. Secondly, we must accept that we live in a multi-cultural and multi-racial society. Although there may be areas of the country where few, if any, ethnic elders currently live, population patterns may change in the coming years; likewise we ourselves may not continue living in the same place.

There is no doubt that, for many of us, addressing this issue may involve us at times in confronting not only others' prejudices but possibly also our own. Sometimes this can be an uncomfortable process, but the results can be enriching and rewarding both for ourselves and for those with whom we work.

Health Related Issues

The warden has a key role to play in terms of advocating good health for those living on the scheme, and in terms of ensuring that residents are not fobbed off by GPs or hospitals by the 'what can you expect at your age' put-down, which we have already considered in this chapter under the section on ageism.

Ill Health and the Ageing Process

What *can* our residents expect? Unequivocally, they have a right to the same treatment and care at 80 years old that they would expect to receive at 20, 30, 40 years old . . . but as we have seen elsewhere in this book, because of stereotypical assumptions and the association of old age with ill health, they often do not receive the care, attention and treatment they deserve.

Ill health is not the inevitable result of ageing; it may accompany the ageing process, but it can and should be treated. The warden, from a basis of distinguishing the difference between the normal ageing process and illness, has a key role to play in encouraging tenants to seek treatment, rather than accepting ill health as something that just has to be put up with.

Equally important is the warden's role in helping residents to maintain good health.

The Warden's Need for Knowledge of Health Issues

In order to carry out these two key elements, wardens need a good working knowledge of the common health problems older people face, together with an understanding of what treatment is available. Additionally, a knowledge of local and national support groups associated with particular conditions – such as the Alzheimer's Disease society, or Arthritis Care, or the Chest, Heart and Stroke Association, for example – means that all available resources can be tapped by the tenant, their relatives and the warden in order to provide support in cases of need.

The issues summarised above are discussed in depth by geriatrician Dr Anne Roberts in her excellent book *A Warden's Guide to Healthcare in Sheltered Housing* (1987). This is essential reading for all wardens, describing clearly good health and illnesses in old age, medicines used by elderly people, what to do in an emergency, frailty in old age (including mental frailty), and terminal illness and bereavement. Throughout the book, the importance of encouraging the independence of tenants is reiterated, and Dr Roberts is one of those (rare) geriatricians with a comprehensive understanding of the warden's role.

Because we encourage all wardens to read Dr Roberts' book we will not attempt to duplicate any of the material here. What we will consider, however, are some practical steps wardens can take which address the issues we have discussed. We will then consider some of the issues surrounding the difficult question of drugs and medication, and the varying requirements of employing organisations regarding the warden's role in this area.

The Six Practical Steps for Wardens

The practical steps a warden can take in terms of the promotion of good health for the elderly are the result of much discussion with wardens over the years. A general consensus is that the following are important areas of practice for wardens:

- to work with tenants in helping them not to accept illness as inevitable, and simply to be put up with;

- to encourage tenants to seek treatment and not be fobbed off by ageist 'what can you expect at your age' remarks;
- to help residents maintain good health, by encouraging good nutrition, for example, or by encouraging them to participate in exercise and activities;
- to act as advocates, ensuring residents are receiving all the benefits to which they are entitled; lack of money or worry about bills etc. can cause or contribute to depression and exacerbate ill health;
- to be clear about the drugs tenants are prescribed, whether or not you are involved in administering them (see next section) but so you can be clear about the conditions that are being treated;
- to have a basic working knowledge of the common illnesses of old age, together with the treatment available, so that you can encourage tenants to seek medical attention.

It can be seen that these steps stem from a commitment to the promotion of good health amongst tenants by wardens. Prerequisites are the basic knowledge we have mentioned, together with the skills of listening, counselling, assertiveness and assessment. Advocacy is a vital aspect of this part of a warden's role and is dealt with separately in this chapter. We have suggested some further reading at the end of this chapter, to supplement the information given in Dr Roberts' book.

Drugs and the Ageing Process

Inappropriately-prescribed Drugs

We have already considered how basic knowledge of the most commonly prescribed medicines can assist a warden in understanding the condition that is being treated. However, this does not imply that there should be an unquestioning acceptance that drugs are always the most appropriate form of treatment. There is evidence to indicate that some of the conditions associated with old age can themselves be the result of inappropriately prescribed drugs or those which are taken in the wrong doses, or combined with medicines left over from a previous prescription. This can be particularly acute in the case of the confused elderly.

In a powerfully argued article in *Social Work Today* (30/6/1988) entitled 'A bitter pill to swallow', social worker Steve

Scrutton looks at this issue. He describes a number of common age-related conditions which often result in social work intervention, including confusion, hypothermia and excessive drowsiness, which may be, in part, the result of medication. He also considers the unquestioning deference given to the medical profession by many older people – and many of us can also identify with this; GPs and hospitals can frequently be intimidating, not set up to regard us as equal partners in our treatment, merely recipients of the service provided.

The article also raises the question of the pressure which is put on doctors to prescribe, and the resulting possibility of problems associated with older people's social and emotional lives being treated with tranquillisers and anti-depressants rather than counselling or care.

Discussion Areas for Wardens

Clearly, wardens are often put in the position of requesting medical attention for their residents, and therefore have a key role to play in ensuring that deeper issues are also considered. When discussing these issues with wardens, they find the ideas put forward in this article particularly thought-provoking.

Fruitful discussion around whether (and how) to challenge the medical profession, and/or to encourage medical intervention often leads to examples which, in turn, take us to the rights/risk debate, considered earlier in this chapter. Many wardens give examples which endorse the argument that drugs cause more problems than they are intended to solve, and the evidence points to the most vulnerable people in this area being the confused elderly.

The Warden's Role in Giving Drugs and Medication

An Anchor research report *Medication in Sheltered Housing* (Adams, Askham, Redfern & Tinker, Anchor 1992) discusses this hitherto largely uncharted topic, following growing concern at wardens' increasing involvement in this area, despite their employers' instructions to the contrary. The study confirms that this is yet another area of potential or actual role conflict for the warden, with tenants' expectations, together with those of district nurses and GPs, that wardens could and should be giving medication conflicting with those of many employers who state that wardens should not become involved in this area. The report found that the wardens included in its sample felt that whilst ordering repeat prescriptions and helping tenants to understand the instructions on their own medication was part of their role, any further involvement – such as giving eye drops or injections, or administering pills and medicines – was not, although the latter might be carried out on an emergency basis. Given the increasing frailty of tenants, more and more wardens are finding themselves in a position where refusal to become involved in this area may mean their tenants suffering, yet compliance with the expectations of some tenants and GPs would mean going against their employer's policies.

The report suggests that, should individual organisations perceive that a change in their policy and thus the warden's role is necessary in this area they should provide both proper training and support, and appropriate insurance cover. Just as the employer must provide clear guidelines to wardens in this area, so wardens must comply with the employer's existing instructions, and must take the initiative and inform the employer if they feel demands are being made beyond the remit of their job, in order to keep managers aware of the extent of the problem. In this way, proper evidence can be provided to enable organisations to review current policies.

References and Further Reading

Adams S, Askham J, Redfern S and Tinker A (1992) *Medication in Sheltered Housing* Oxford: Anchor Housing Trust.

Age Concern (1984) Housing and related problems among elders in ethnic minorities

Blair, Pat (1991) *Know Your Medicines* Age Concern.

Butler A and Pritchard C (1983) *Social Work and Mental Illness* London: Macmillan Press Ltd.

Froggat A (1990) *Family Work with Elderly People* Basingstoke: Macmillan Education Ltd.

Lawrence J (1988) 'The Myths of Old Age' in *New Society* 18 March 1988, pp 19–21.

Marshall M (1983) *Social Work with Old People* Basingstoke: Macmillan Education Ltd.

Marshall M (ed) (1990) *Working with Dementia* Birmingham: Venture Press.

National Federation of Housing Associations (1982) *Race and Housing: A Guide for Housing Associations* London, NFHA.

Neill J (1989) *Assessing Elderly People for Residential Care: A Practical Guide* London: National Institute for Social Work.

Norman A (1987) *Aspects of Ageism: A Discussion paper* London: Centre for Policy on Ageing.

Norman A (1981) *Rights and Risks* London: Centre for Policy on Ageing.

Norman A (1985) *Triple Jeopardy: growing old in a second homeland* London: Centre for Policy on Ageing.
Roberts, Dr Anne (1987) *A Wardens Guide to Healthcare in Sheltered Housing* Surrey: Age Concern, England.
Scrutton S (1988) A Bitter Pill to Swallow in *Social Work Today* 30.6.1988.
Scrutton S (1989) *Counselling Older People, A Creative Response to Ageing* London: Edward Arnold (excellent on ageism).
Stevenson O (1989) *Age and Vulnerability, A Guide to Better Care* London: Edward Arnold.
Stott M (1973) Age Old Problem in the *Guardian* 22.11.73 (on ageism).
Whitehorn K (1973) Don't tell me the old, old story, in the *Observer* 9.12.73 (on ageism).
White Paper (1989) *Caring for People: Community Care into the next Decade and Beyond* (Cmd 849) London: HMSO.

CHAPTER 6
The Warden as Manager

Introduction

Now, more than ever before, there is a need for wider recognition of just how complex the nature of the warden's job actually is – the skills used each day, the knowledge needed to do the job, and how those skills and knowledge are applied in order to benefit and maximise the potential of each resident. This chapter is intended to discuss the concept of the warden as professional worker, manager of care services for tenants, whose status and role should be regarded as being on a par with colleagues also working with their clients, such as District Nurses, Home Care Organisers, Health Visitors and Social Workers.

At the moment, probably as a result of the somewhat *ad hoc* history of the role of the warden as discussed in Chapter 1, there is still a lack of clarity generally about the role and status of the warden. The job is not immediately recognised as that of a professional, although those with a clear understanding of what the job is about can see that the same management skills and techniques as are learnt and applied by colleagues in other professions are vital to the warden. The development of the National Certificated Course and now the Advanced Certificated Course for wardens, with their focus on the development of professional skills and management techniques, have greatly assisted the process of increased recognition of the training and educational needs of the warden. As the care-in-the-community initiatives are implemented and wardens are recognised as key managers of care for their residents by workers from the health and social services departments, a clearer public image is emerging.

One Model for the Future

In their excellent booklet *Sheltered Housing in the 1990s* Anchor Housing Association explain the positive policies they have developed for sheltered housing in the light of care in the community; these will enable wardens to manage care for their frailer tenants and allow Anchor to develop care partnerships with local authorities, meeting the needs of the local community by maximising the potential of sheltered housing to support the vulnerable older people living in the local community. They argue that 'traditionally, wardens in sheltered housing schemes have been viewed as no more than a "good neighbour" and their support role was vague and unclear'. Anchor has clearly defined their perception of the warden's role and describes the main job tasks as follows:

- Identifying care needs;
- Referring to the statutory services;
- Acting as key worker once a care plan is in place;
- Representing the tenant, monitoring and reviewing services and care needs;
- Providing hands on care in specific circumstances, emergency or planned short term care.

The formulation and publication of these policies show that Anchor wardens are equipped with management back-up to carry out the role of key worker or care manager for their tenants. Short term hands-on care is only to be provided in clearly-defined specific circumstances; for most of the time, the warden's role is to ensure that the necessary care is provided. This is an endorsement of what the majority of wardens – and many, though sadly, not all, warden's employers – have always considered the role to rightfully be. Anchor, with its national profile have made a great contribution towards the professionalism of working within sheltered housing, and it is to be hoped that other employers will follow this lead.

For wardens still struggling, unsupported, with the challenges they face, it is not so easy to make the leap from unclear, ill-defined 'good neighbour' to professional worker, however desirable it may seem to do so. Nevertheless, the process of recognition must begin with wardens themselves.

Beyond the 'Good Neighbour' Concept

Whether the warden is involved in managing the care for an individual resident, or planning and organising a scheme-wide activity, be it recreational, educational or welfare-based, management skills are put into practice every day. Yet, from what wardens tell us, there are still those whose perception of the warden has not yet progressed beyond that of the good neighbour, needing little or no support and training. We have seen how inappropriate and outmoded this is, and simply by examining the replies to some very basic questions we can provide good evidence that wardens do indeed operate at a management level.

The first question to be addressed is the *amount of day-to-day supervision* wardens generally receive – the answer to which is, in most cases, very little or none at all. When we ask wardens the direct question: 'Who tells you what to do every day?' the answer is most likely to be that no one does, or ever has done; they decide for themselves, and that decision is based on a number of factors, including the immediate needs of their tenants combined with things they had planned or intended to do as part of a routine which they themselves had set up. This level of independence is comparable with that of senior managers; and when we ask our second question about the *frequency with which wardens see their own managers*, and receive the reply that such contacts are few and far between, this further reinforces the principle of autonomy. Indeed, the majority of managers working within Housing Organisations or in Social Services Departments have far more contact with, and therefore guidance from, their own bosses than wardens do; wardens operate for much of the time at a level of autonomy that would be unthinkable for other staff at similar levels working elsewhere within the employing organisation.

Our third question concerns the *resources that wardens manage* – or, in other words, have responsibility for. All wardens reply that they have responsibility, to a greater or lesser extent, for people and in particular for tenants; for the bricks and mortar of their schemes; for the social and community factors within their schemes; for their workload; for their time; and for themselves; and many also add a responsibility for managing staff (deputies, reliefs, cleaning staff) and budgets.

Finally, we ask wardens about the *level of decision making* that is required of them. Without exception, all wardens report making decisions which deeply affect people's lives, not just occasionally but as a regular and continuing part of their jobs. Added to these of course are a million and one other types of decisions which wardens have to make associated with the health and welfare of their tenants, and the smooth and effective running of the sheltered housing scheme. Quite clearly, a further factor in the decision-making process operated by the warden may be the necessity to make a decision to step back from a particular situation – not to opt out, rather to deliberately take no action in order to encourage action to emanate from elsewhere.

It can clearly be seen that many complex factors have to be weighed up by the warden during the course of making any decision – yet frequently the nature of the decisions mean that they cannot be pondered over, or even discussed with colleagues, or made with guidance from senior managers – they call for immediate judgement, followed by immediate action.

The results of all four questions can be summarised by saying that wardens are semi-autonomous, receiving little or no day-to-day supervision or guidance from their own managers. They organise their own workload, have responsibility for major resources including people and bricks and mortar, and they make far-reaching decisions which affect people's lives during the every day course of their work. Apply these criteria to a manager as perceived in the traditional sense of the word, and we can see the similarities. Following this exercise, many wardens have pointed out to us that the major differences between themselves and their own senior management are pay and status!

Management Techniques for Wardens

Having considered these points, it naturally follows that an enhanced understanding of the management process through consideration of some basic, yet essential, management skills and techniques can help wardens to recognise and reinforce their abilities as managers. This is an aspect of the increase in self-awareness and opportunity for self development which are themes running through this book; although the skills and activities described are probably already being put into practice, nevertheless recognising, reviewing and developing areas of work which may previously have been taken for granted can greatly increase confidence, self-esteem and ultimately, it is hoped, professionalism.

We shall consider the following management techniques:

- defining objectives;
- setting priorities;
- decision making;
- planning and organising;
- reviewing and monitoring;
- time management;
- delegation;
- information systems/record keeping, including access to records.

This is by no means an exhaustive list of management skills but these are the ones which seem to relate most closely to the warden's job. Communication skills, which are fundamental to good management, are not considered separately here, since we have examined them in depth in Chapter 4. However, it is important to regard the specific management techniques we cover in this chapter as being underpinned by the skills of listening, questioning, counselling and assertiveness together with confident written communication skills.

Defining Objectives

Without necessarily being conscious of the fact, wardens set objectives for themselves, their schemes and their residents on a continuous basis. A more formal recognition of this process can help both in the planning and meeting of these objectives. It may help to think of objectives as goals or targets to be reached, relevant to all aspects of running a sheltered housing scheme, whether it is formulating an individual care plan for a particular tenant, or planning the programme of scheme events for the year ahead. It is not only necessary to be clear about the target in each case, but the realistic timescale within which that target can be met must also be part of the planning process.

When addressing this aspect of management with groups of wardens, they have found it helpful to apply this technique to the hypothetical situation of setting up a completely new sheltered housing scheme. The task is to set three objectives, one short-term (within the first week) one medium-term (within the first month) and one long-term objective (within the first year). Discussion about this is always fast and furious, since everyone has their own priorities; but a consensus is often reached along the following lines:

Short-term objective: (first week) — obtain all relevant necessary information about the new tenants;

Medium-term objective: (first month) — arrange a social activity in the common room to enable residents to begin to get to know each other;

Long-term objective: (first year) — encourage the establishment of a residents' committee which would organise activities and events for the scheme as a whole.

(No doubt everyone reading this will have their own strongly held views about this, and may feel other things should take priority, but one of the rewards of the warden's job is the autonomy to make such decisions!)

It can be seen that, once goals are clearly identified, with a realistic timescale, it becomes easier to work towards them with a sense of purpose. To use some jargon, this could be described as being 'pro-active'. Pro-activity could be described as not only the attempt to foresee or plan events in advance, but to create a situation in which you can have some influence over how, or whether, those events will happen. To be 'reactive', on the other hand, is to wait until the event takes place and react accordingly. Many wardens feel that the nature of the job imposes a degree of reactivity, given that much of the work is about responding to residents' needs and demands. However, as we shall see when we consider this alongside time management, planning and monitoring and setting priorities, it is not only possible but also highly beneficial to everyone concerned for the warden to run the scheme in as pro-active a way as possible.

Setting Priorities

Wardens are constantly reorganising their priorities; they may begin the day with a series of clear targets or objectives in mind, together with the relative importance of each, yet within the first half an hour some event occurs which means they have to re-assess their plan for the whole day in the light of the attention and time which now needs to be given to this new issue. One set of criteria which can be applied to each event in order to help prioritise it is whether it is urgent but not important; important but not urgent; or both urgent AND important.

Something which is urgent but not important might be dealt with first, quickly, without allocating too much time to it; an issue which is important but not urgent can be addressed later, when more time is available to concentrate on it. Something which is both urgent AND important will take priority over both of these and will need a proportionate amount of time spent on it. When we have discussed this with groups of wardens they are eager to share examples of events or issues which fit these criteria and to discuss how easy it is to concentrate too much time on the most immediately demanding task whether or not it could be counted as really important. The application of these three criteria therefore, can not only help with setting priorities but is also crucially linked with a more productive use of time.

Time Management

Many wardens feel that this is a particularly difficult area for them, given how much of their job actually involves responding to emergencies or unforeseeable situations. Time management could be defined as the skill of organising yourself in advance and allocating time to each area of your job in a balanced way; in terms of the warden's role it means there is a need to schedule time to be pro-active, or in other words to work towards your short-, medium- and long-term goals, whilst ensuring that time is also available for dealing with the every-day running problems, or the re-active tasks. It can be seen here that an understanding of the difference between urgency and importance plays a fundamental role in allocating and managing time.

Many wardens have suggested that a more logical approach to the management of time on their part has led to their residents gradually being able to distinguish between issues which demand the warden's immediate attention and issues which can wait until later to be discussed – the warden having allocated a particular part of the day to be available for residents to talk over problems which can wait.

Wardens who work in this way feel it is important to use all available resources to inform residents of their hours of duty, timetable and routine – a calendar for the week or month, notices, newsletters; any method which reinforces that there is a plan for the day and beyond, and a methodical approach to managing the scheme.

Additional tools which assist in time management, along with defining objectives and setting priorities, are year planners and diaries. Year planners can help with long term objective setting – the summer outings, the Christmas party, the jumble sale – whilst recording the regular or planned events which take place, either in the common room – the fortnightly coffee morning, the keep fit class which takes place only during the academic terms for example – or elsewhere, such as the warden's attendance on a course or annual leave. Both warden and residents can find this useful; it certainly helps with scheduling time in a pro-active fashion.

Diaries are often used retrospectively by wardens rather than as planning tools for the future. In other words they are used to keep a record of what happened, visits made to residents, action taken, medication prescribed, emergencies that occurred and so on. Such information is of course important to record, particularly if it is used by a deputy, mobile or relief warden and it is also vital as a record of action taken on behalf of a particular resident should it be necessary to prove this later on. The scheme diary however is not the appropriate place for keeping these records, for both legal and practical reasons (see 'Information Systems, Record Keeping and Access to Records' later in this chapter). Quite apart from the ethical issues associated with keeping confidential information in this way, it means that the diary is a somewhat jumbled combination of past and present, which does not help with planning for the future.

Diaries as a method of planning future time are crucial to time management. To assist with such planning however they can be the appropriate place in which to keep some records, such as maintenance visits – the servicing of fire alarm or fire fighting equipment, for example, so the intervals between such visits can be properly monitored. Used effectively however, diaries enable you to plan what is going to happen rather than to record what has already taken place.

Decision Making

Wardens make decisions every day of their working lives. Separating out decision making from the management skills already discussed is a difficult task, for in order to define objectives and set priorities for a scheme, or for a particular resident, a number of alternative ideas have to be considered, sifted, weighed up and then either adopted or rejected depending upon the chosen criteria. The decisions that are the easiest to make are often those where plenty of time is available to ponder over them. Harder decisions will be those which are made on the spot, in an emergency situation for example, where it may be necessary to weigh up the alternative courses of action at lightning speed, and then choose one of them.

Wardens often say that, with hindsight, they feel they may not have made the 'right' decision in such cases. However, there is little doubt that they made the best decision possible in view of the circumstances. An interesting exercise we have carried out is to present small groups of wardens with case studies of emergency situations and ask them what decision they would make, and why. Feedback almost always shows that there are no set 'right answers'; each group prepares a response to the situation, which turns out to be different from that of the other participating groups, and yet equally valid and justifiable. The outcome of this exercise is both comforting and illuminating, since it clearly shows that there is frequently no one course of action that is 'right'; rather there are often a number of alternative scenarios and options which could be considered relevant and appropriate in the circumstances.

This issue is discussed in greater depth in Chapter 7 in relation to Health and Safety issues, and in Chapter 5, where we consider medication and drugs. Suffice it to say that, for a warden, decision making is a fundamental part of the role, yet one which, sadly, is not always recognised by others.

Planning and Organising

Again this is inextricably linked with the foregoing management techniques. It could perhaps be described as the fine detail of achieving the targets or goals you have set. Allocating time to planning activities – a pro-active use of time – will help to ensure the target is met through the best use of resources and with as little wasted effort as possible. Wardens often suggest a method that works for them as first brainstorming (or listing in no particular order) every task which needs to be carried out in order to achieve a particular target, and then going back over the list to put each action item in a logical sequence. Many wardens express the sense of satisfaction to be gained in ticking off each task as it is completed – and also find it easier to see whether certain areas or tasks can be delegated (see below). A more sophisticated form of this technique is known as 'critical path analysis'; it is a recognised and useful management tool, which, adapted in this simple way, can help in the planning of complex tasks or projects.

Reviewing and Monitoring

What went right? Note it down to do it again in the future. What went wrong? Why? Analyse, and again note for future reference. Reviewing can be usefully carried out after each one-off event, or each set of complex tasks which have to be completed regularly. Monitoring, or keeping a general eye on how things are going, as well as helping wardens to gain an overall perspective on the scheme, can also help them to see how far they are achieving their long-term objectives, and whether priorities need to be reassessed in view of current developments or anticipated future changes.

Delegation

Wardens, especially those who do not directly supervise staff, often feel that they have no one to whom to delegate. Because they work in isolation with a client group experiencing increasing frailty there is sometimes a feeling that there is no-one but themselves to undertake increasing numbers of care tasks for their tenants, until for some, the workload feels almost unbearable.

One helpful approach to this feeling for some wardens can be a reminder that they are not employed to do everything for everyone – rather, it is the warden's role to *see that things get done*. This is the role Anchor have defined as being the 'key worker', identifying care needs, and facilitating the care plan once it is in place. It does of course, imply that there are people, services and facilities available to enable the care plan to be implemented – home carers, district nurses, relatives (who may have to be reminded that it is not the warden's role to provide hands-on care on anything other than a short-term, emergency basis). In other words, wardens do have a range of people to whom they can delegate – and we could add the tenants themselves and their relatives to that list, together with cleaners, caretakers, mobile or relief wardens, some of whose work wardens may find themselves doing because it is, in the short term perhaps 'easier' or 'quicker' to do it themselves! This is of course a very easy trap to fall into, but the long-term effects of this approach are of course negative; the burden of stress it places upon the warden must be considered, together with the raised expectations of tenants and their relatives. Finally, in the very longest term, we must consider whether the fact that the warden may be prepared to carry out services that should rightfully be provided by others means that resources could be directed away from sheltered housing as a policy decision 'because the warden is there' – the TWIT syndrome, which we first considered in Chapter 1.

We can see, therefore, how crucial it is for wardens to fully understand the need for delegation. As well as understanding to whom to delegate, it will be necessary to consider how to do it; for this the skill of assertiveness is paramount and this is discussed in depth in Chapter 4. Management support may also be needed, particularly if the warden makes a conscious decision to change approach, and perhaps also to add weight to the warden's requests for input from other services. The relationship between wardens and management is discussed in Chapter 7.

Information Systems, Record Keeping and Access to Records

The keeping of comprehensive and clear records on each client is an integral element of managing the sheltered scheme effectively.

The introduction of alarm systems linked to central control throughout the 1980s meant that some of the previous somewhat casual and *ad hoc* practices with regard to recording essential information concerning tenants had to be replaced by a more formal system that could be quickly and easily referred to by mobile or visiting wardens and perhaps also control-centre staff.

More sophisticated technology meant that tenants' records were entered into computer information systems, so that as soon as a tenant made a call to the control centre, vital information regarding issues such as their age, state of health, next of kin, when last visited and by whom, whether the doctor was called etc. could be retrieved immediately by staff having no previous knowledge of that tenant. In turn this meant that action taken on behalf of that tenant in the absence of the warden could be based on full and current information; and the system continuously up-dated so everyone could be aware of the present situation regarding each individual on the scheme.

Prior to this, much of the information regarding tenants was often held in the warden's own head – she or he knowing each resident so well that written records may have seemed unnecessary, and handover time to deputy or relief wardens needing only a quick verbal briefing, since they, too, probably knew each resident and their problems only too well. Any significant action taken on behalf of a tenant would be recorded in the daily diary.

However, as the role of the warden has gradually changed, evolved and developed over the years, so has the need for efficient information systems. This has been underlined by legislation. The Data Protection Act 1984 gives everyone the right to see records about themselves that are kept on computers. In addition, your residents now have a legal right to see what is recorded about them, following the Access to Personal Files Act 1987. This Act, which came into force in 1989, defines the obligation to give access to records made by housing and social services departments of local authorities. This includes records on residents kept by wardens, and has implications for how such information should be recorded. Records should be secure; they must be dated and signed; they must be factual, succinct, truthful, and, if opinions are expressed, they should be substantiated by facts. Remember that, whilst your residents have a legal right to see what you have written about them, they may not see what a third party has written, unless permission has been given.

Your employer may well already have provided you with some specific training in this area, along with making tenants aware of these legislative changes. If you are still unclear, ask your manager for clarification, and see Cornwell (1990) and Fielding (1989) in the 'Further Reading' section for discussion of these issues.

Therefore we can see the need for a clear and efficient scheme-based record system which anyone who has the right of access can turn to and understand immediately. This means that the old fashioned, but in many cases, still current, method of recording everything that happens to the scheme and to individual residents in a rather jumbled up version of events in the diary is no longer appropriate. Information regarding residents must be kept separately, and securely, and if one resident wishes to see what has been written about them they must not be able to see information regarding others at the same time. You, or the relief or mobile warden, can have instant access to records concerning individuals, without having to search through pages of irrelevant information; and your diary can be properly used as a tool in the management and planning process for your scheme.

Conclusions

Without doubt, many wardens are already organising their work in some of the ways we have looked at. However, feedback from the many groups of wardens with whom we have considered these issues indicates that an increased awareness of themselves as managers, in part through a greater understanding of management techniques and their relevance to the role of the warden, can mean a significant and positive difference in wardens' own attitudes towards themselves and to their job. Consideration of these skills can be a way of validating and confirming what is already taking place; it can also provide opportunities for re-appraising working methods and for evaluating and considering new approaches more consistent with concept of the warden as care manager, or key worker – the professional scheme based co-ordinator of services for older people.

From this self-recognition should follow recognition by others – employers, colleagues both within the organisation and outside, and others involved in providing services and care for the elderly.

References and Further Reading

Anchor Housing Association (1990) *Sheltered Housing in the 1990s: the positive choice* Oxford: Anchor H.A.

Cornwell N (1990) On Record and Open to Question in *Social Work Today*, 18 January 1990, pp 28–29 (on access to records).

Fielding N (1989) Laying our cards on the table *Community Care* 4 May 1989, pp 24–25 (on access to records).

Handy, Charles (3rd Edition 1986) *Understanding Organisations* Penguin.

Mulligan, John (1988) *The Personal Management Handbook* London: Sphere.

Pedler M and Boydell T (1985) *Managing Yourself* London: Fontana/Collins.

CHAPTER 7 Managing Sheltered Housing

Introduction

Having considered the management skills used by the warden in the previous chapter, let us now look at some of the major aspects of running a sheltered housing scheme which utilise these skills in conjunction with the communication skills discussed in Chapter 4. Managing a sheltered housing complex is often a balancing act between having responsibility for the management of care for individuals and considering the wider needs of the whole community living on the scheme.

As we have seen, such a balancing act can sometimes appear to be a series of conflicting demands. The task facing the warden is to use their skills to best effect. This can involve dealing with a range of areas including making decisions about resources, negotiating with suppliers of services, and creating effective communication links in order to gain support.

Some of the key areas in which you will be called upon to exercise these skills will be in addressing issues surrounding medical and other emergencies, Health and Safety and fire safety; in the encouragement of the effective use of any communal resources you may have on your complex; and in the process of settling in new tenants to your scheme. This chapter therefore will enable you to examine your role in these areas. Given that your individual employers will have widely differing views and expectations of you with regard to each one of them, we can only look here at the fundamental principles associated with each one, giving examples of good practice wherever possible, or appropriate. You will need to apply the general principles to your own particular employing organisation's policies and practices. In many cases, especially regarding areas such as medical emergencies, Health and Safety and fire safety, the message is that you may need to ask for clarification from your employer as to the application of the appropriate legislation in your scheme, or for further explanation of policies determined centrally, which directly affect your working practices. We discuss general aspects relating to each of these areas which may help to set the agenda for any discussions that you may have with your employer, or to formulate the questions that you might need to ask.

We consider the relationship between wardens and their own managers. In order to manage the sheltered scheme effectively wardens need to feel confident and comfortable with their line managers, knowing that clear guidance will be available at all times, ideally through regular one-to-one support, a programme of wardens meetings, and an up-to-date wardens manual or handbook, giving clear guidelines on organisational policies and practices.

Finally, we consider the recently proposed 'Code of Practice for Wardens', designed to provide a common set of values and expectations within which wardens can carry out their jobs effectively.

Dealing with Emergencies

First Aid and Lifting

Many of the original job descriptions issued to wardens contained the expectation that they would be able to provide first aid in emergency situations concerning their tenants. Employers were not always specific about the qualifications needed – some appointed former nurses, expecting that they would be best able to cope in situations such as burns, bleeding, heart attacks and strokes. Others asked for an up-to-date St John Ambulance or Red Cross First Aid Certificate, or sponsored their employee to take a course leading to such a certificate.

Some employers continue to expect that wardens will provide first aid, whilst others have clearly discouraged staff from doing so. The reasons for this change in attitude are not always clear, and those wardens who have specifically been instructed not to apply first aid techniques often feel they are in an invidious position. How could they stand by and watch a tenant bleed to death from an artery, they ask, without taking some action to halt the bleeding? Wardens are practical people, with common sense and a caring attitude towards their tenants, and therefore complying with their employers' instructions can be very difficult. Asking the employer for clear guidance in this area is important – and it is equally vital that tenants and relatives are informed by management as to the scope and limit of the warden's role in this regard.

We have all heard of the well meaning first-aider (probably an amateur, or someone without an up-to-date qualification) whose action has caused more problems than it has solved. The possibility of this happening in sheltered housing and relatives suing the employing organisation as a result, is probably one of the reasons why employers are now instructing staff not to take action. Additionally, employers are now concerned regarding cross-infection through blood or body fluids, and whilst they issue gloves, aprons etc., to be used by employees whose role it is to provide 'hands on' personal care in their day-to-day work, they are concerned to limit such possibilities wherever they can.

The First Aid At Work Regulations (1981) made it clear that employers had a duty to provide first aid facilities at work for their employees. This generally involved organisations training a certain number of employees in first aid techniques, and designating them as a recognised First-Aider. However, no legislation exists to cover the administration of first aid and to people not actually in their employment – therefore there is no obligation to provide first aid to the tenants of sheltered housing. Once these regulations were in place, many employers took the opportunity to reconsider the necessity to employ first-aiders or to train wardens in first aid.

A further factor affecting employers' reservations about their staff applying first aid techniques is that many of them involve lifting. In view of the need to understand how to do this properly in order not to place a strain on the back, and considering the number of back injuries that take place in the workplace every year, employers are naturally reluctant for staff without formal training in this area to carry out this activity.

Some employing organisations instruct staff not to undertake any lifting at all. Many wardens have expressed the view that it is all very well to be instructed or advised not to lift, but to wait for help to arrive – but in these times of scarce resources, and with a tenant who falls frequently, or needs raising up in bed, many wardens feel they are placed in a very difficult position if they are unable to undertake this task. However, to lift without being properly trained in the correct techniques can cause far more long-term problems than the short-term problem it solves. Therefore, if, either implicitly of explicitly, it is a requirement of your job to lift tenants from time to time, you should ensure that you are properly trained by your employer to do so.

The guidance that is often given to wardens therefore is that when a medical emergency occurs, the warden must 'make the person comfortable' whilst summoning the ambulance or GP. This is where the warden's skills of assessment and decision making are paramount. Whatever action is taken – or not taken

– can have far-reaching effects on the life of the tenant currently at risk through a medical emergency. It is vital to obtain clarification of exactly what is meant by 'making the person comfortable'. Does it mean covering them with a blanket, for example, in order that loss of body heat through shock is minimised? Does it mean placing an unconscious, or semi-conscious person into the recovery position? If so, clearly an immediate assessment must be made as to whether any bones may be broken before moving them.

The issue for those employers who do expect their wardens to possess a current first aid certificate is of course that it raises the expectations of tenants that appropriate first aid techniques will be applied as necessary. This, as we have already seen, creates a problem should the first-aider misjudge the situation; it also creates the necessity for anyone who deputises for the warden at any time needing to have the same skills and knowledge. This is perhaps not such a problem for a large organisation having the resources to provide an on-going training programme in first aid qualifications for all resident, relief and mobile wardens. It might, however, present difficulties for those organisations with fewer resources, whose relief or deputy warden may be a part-time member of staff, or even a tenant. Clearly, those wardens working within such organisations must be clear as to what is expected, just as it must be made explicit to tenants what they can expect in the way of the administration of first aid.

Whilst there may be no explicit aspect of the job description that requires the warden to provide first aid, there may be phrases in which it is implicit. If this is the case, clarification of what is implied must be obtained from employers, both for the warden's owns benefit and for that of tenants and their relatives.

Whatever the case with regard to the employers' requirements in this area, any information given to tenants and their relatives by the employing organisation regarding the wardens duties must make absolutely clear the limits of the wardens' role, in order not to create unrealistic expectations.

Non-Medical Emergencies

Emergencies are of course not always medical in nature, although perhaps these are the most commonly experienced in sheltered housing. When discussing the range of situations that could be described as emergencies with a group of wardens, they have ranged from one resident threatening another with a knife; a flood or fire on the scheme; a series of burglaries on the complex occurring whilst warden and tenants were out on a coach trip; a confused resident being left behind at the seaside whilst on an outing, and the discovery not being made until the coach was half way home; and a complete loss of heat and light to a sheltered complex for some hours on a cold winter's night. What these situations all have in common is the need to assess the situation and to make a series of decisions quickly; peoples' lives are affected, both by what has happened and by the warden's subsequent handling of the situation.

When discussing such instances with groups of wardens, an exercise that is often helpful is for pairs or small groups to discuss each incident without knowing the outcome, or what action the warden concerned actually took. What would group members have done in similar circumstances? How would they have dealt with the situation? Groups are given two minutes for this. Frequently each group comes up with a slightly different approach to each situation, illustrating that there is no definitive right way to deal with such diverse occurrences; the warden is called upon to deploy many of the management skills and techniques we have discussed earlier, including setting priorities, delegation, and time management, in addition to assessment and decision making. Moreover, these are required to be utilised very quickly.

There is not the opportunity to mull things over, let alone to discuss the situation with a colleague or ask the manager for guidance. Action taken in such situations can only be based on the use of these skills and based upon the information available at the time. Luckily, wardens are very good at such split-second timing, and such situations are generally dealt with coolly, calmly and competently.

However, what sometimes happens after such incidents is that, over the following days or weeks, wardens berate themselves with questions about why they did not take more or different, action, failing to give themselves credit for the positive aspects of the way they handled the situation. We can all use the benefit of hindsight and the opportunity to consider in depth the various options that could be taken; this is why, when carrying out the group exercise, each group is given only two minutes to come to a decision, as this is more like the reality of the situations they will encounter.

Such situations are very stressful for the warden, who needs therefore, to have an opportunity to de-brief afterwards. Preferably this should be to someone who will quietly and constructively listen, without being in any way judgemental, or try to 'top' the story by recounting a similar but, in their view, even worse incident. Access to a co-listener in such circumstances is important – see Chapter 4 for more about listening and counselling. Further information about the recording and reporting of both medical and non-medical emergencies can be found in the next section on Health and Safety.

Health and Safety Matters

Employers Responsibility

Under the Health and Safety at Work (HASW) Act 1974 Section 2, paragraph 2 (c), employers have an unequivocal responsibility for the provision of information, instruction, training and supervision in order to ensure the health and safety at work of their employees. Apart from some shining exceptions we have come across, there is no doubt that many wardens feel untrained, uninstructed and unsupported in this area. This probably has much to do with the location of the workplace – sheltered schemes do not form part of the employer's central offices, and therefore are often left out when it comes to health and safety inspections. Health and Safety reps in the workplace may not even be aware of the existence of sheltered schemes unless the wardens themselves, or the wardens' line manager, draw attention to them.

Nevertheless, not only are your health, safety and welfare at work protected in law under the 1974 HASW Act, so in turn do you have a responsibility to look after yourself and others. You, the warden, have a 'duty to care' for the residents living on your complex. Just as your employer must ensure that the sheltered scheme is a safe workplace for you, so you have a day-to-day management responsibility for the safety of the common parts of your complex. In this way, the working environment is healthy and safe for you, for your tenants, their relatives and visitors, and others who may work at or visit the complex from time to time.

One area that causes problems for wardens and their employers is that of tenants' own flats. Many wardens have a duty to enter tenants' homes, as part of their job. If they do so, and it is expected of them by their employer either implicitly or explicitly, then the individual tenant's home is also the warden's workplace. However, at the same time it must be recognised that wardens' employers have no power over what individual tenants choose to do in their homes. As the warden you can give advice to tenants on potential hazards; if you consider someone's home presents a danger to you, or others who might enter it, you should discuss this with the tenant concerned whilst also reporting it in writing to your manager. We must remember, of course, that individuals have a right to put themselves at risk if they wish; we are concerned here with whether their actions may put you or others at risk also.

If you consider that you have not received sufficient instruction or training with regard to health and safety matters in your scheme then you are entitled to request that your employer provides this. Ideally each scheme should have its own written guidelines in terms of health and safety policies, which you, the warden should be consulted upon – preferably you should be involved in writing them. If you work for a large employer such as a Borough Council, there may be a Safety Section or an Occupational Health section on whom your manager could call for guidance. If you work for a smaller organisation, the local office of the Health and Safety Executive – which exists to ensure that the legislation enshrined within the 1974 HASW Act is put into practice – will provide support and guidance to your management and to you.

The Wardens Role

The warden's role with regard to Health and Safety matters can be divided into two main areas – a monitoring and reporting role, which can also include taking action to avoid potential accidents and hazards, and dealing directly with accidents and incidents, which also involves a reporting function.

Monitoring and Reporting

You have a duty to monitor the state of repair of all carpets, electric leads and flexes, flooring, staircases, banisters etc., etc. in the common parts of your scheme

You should record and report all faults, and keep chasing them until the problem is resolved. If necessary, you might have to temporarily make good if you can, or keep the area clear in order to avoid accidents.

When contractors are on site you should first of all ensure that they make themselves known to you by showing some identification. Whilst they are carrying out their work, if you consider their methods of working to be unsafe, tell them – and tell your manager also, reporting any unsatisfactory practice in writing. If contractors are to be on site for any length of time, such as for major works, try to ensure you have an out-of-hours telephone number in case of emergency. You should be included in site meetings, but wardens are occasionally forgotten, so use your assertiveness to ensure you are both included and listened to.

Accidents and Injuries
When dealing with any accident or incident that might occur on your scheme, initial assessment of the situation should include consideration of whether any action you propose to take would put yourself, or the person concerned at risk. Accidents and injuries often cover the kinds of situations we have already looked at under medical and non-medical emergencies; situations where people's lives are at risk or where an accident, incident or injury has occurred in the workplace. Remember particularly that any incidence of violence or abusive behaviour against you, the warden, must be reported. We have heard from many wardens about being physically or verbally threatened, or actually attacked by residents – the kind of behaviour that would not be tolerated for a moment in the organisation's office, yet which is sometimes ignored when it happens on a sheltered scheme. To make things worse, of course, the scheme is also the resident warden's home, giving no respite from the environment where the incident took place. In order for such events to be dealt with, they must be reported, in writing, to management

It is good practice for all employers to maintain a record of all dangerous occurrences affecting their employees and others who may work, live on or visit their premises.

A dangerous occurrence can include accidents where injury occurs, however slight; incidents that could have caused injury – 'near misses'; and verbal threats, where the risk of injury is feared – or indeed actual violence against an employee, as we have already considered. Such records serve various functions. They enable a picture to be gained of how dangerous an area might be, by the number and severity of occurrences; they can form a legal protection against claims not related to the occurrence; and they are required by law.

The Reporting of Industrial Diseases and Dangerous Occurrences Regulations 1985 demand that certain illnesses and incidents are reported to the Health and Safety Executive on Form F2508. In order for an employer to make such reports, the warden must provide the appropriate information. In turn, the employer has a duty to ensure that wardens are clear about the reporting system.

An Accident Record Book must also be kept. This can be an internally kept record, and part of the employers' own system of record keeping. However, in addition to this, a DHSS Accident

Book B1 510 must also be available for all employees, which is used to record incidents where a claim of Industrial Injury Benefit may be made. In practice, all injuries should be recorded here in case, at some future stage, a debilitating condition occurs which could be linked to the original accident.

If you feel at all unclear about your responsibilities for Health and Safety within your scheme you should not hesitate to ask your line manager for guidance. Remember that, in order to carry out your own responsibilities, you are entitled to proper training and guidance from your employing organisation.

Food Hygiene

Where wardens have responsibility for any kind of communal catering, this work is covered by the Food Hygiene (General) Regulations 1970. As in the previous section, it is the employer's duty to ensure that wardens comply with these. Food must be prepared and handled with regard for basic safety and hygiene, and employers must both inform and train in this area.

A common misconception regarding these regulations is that they apply only to restaurants, canteens etc. However, they also apply to wardens preparing afternoon teas, the annual Christmas lunch, or the sandwiches for the jumble sale in the communal kitchen of the sheltered complex. The regulations would not apply if these tasks were delegated to residents who prepared the food in their own homes; however, if the warden, as a paid employee, was involved as well then the legislation would apply.

Wardens who have undertaken basic food hygiene training have reported that much of it is based around common-sense practices, and that they have learnt about issues which were new to them and which they can apply in their own kitchens at home as well as to the preparation of food for events on the complex. The local Environmental Health Department will help and advise any organisation needing support in this area, and wardens may want to approach them, in conjunction with their managers, if their employing organisation cannot provide the necessary training directly.

Fire Safety

Wardens have a crucial role to play with regard to fire safety on their sheltered schemes. The guidance as to what action to take in the event of a fire will vary between employing organisations and between complexes, and will depend upon the view held by the organisation's Fire Safety officer (if there is one) or upon the advice of the local Fire Brigade.

In addition to fire action, the other two key areas for wardens to consider are fire prevention, and fire preparation.

Fire Prevention

Fire prevention is about ensuring that the sheltered housing scheme is managed with regard to fire safety at all times. You should familiarise yourself with all the firefighting equipment that is in your scheme. Ask your manager for practical training in the use of the different types of fire extinguishers. Understand when to use which type.

Fire equipment should be inspected and tested regularly, normally by a contractor. You can play your part in ensuring this is done satisfactorily by recording the date and result of the inspection, and, if a fault is found, by noting when it is dealt with.

It is helpful to sound the fire alarm, briefly each week, to test it and to familiarise tenants with its sound. You should be familiar with the zones in the building as indicated on the fire alarm panel.

Doors are a vitally important first line of defence, preventing the spread of fire and smoke. They must be well maintained, and the notices on them properly observed.

All doors must be kept clear of obstructions at all times. They should never under any circumstances by wedged open.

Store and electrical cupboard doors must be kept locked shut. They should normally carry notices to this effect.

Cross-corridor doors having magnetic holders which keep them open during the day, will close automatically when the fire alarm sounds. They should be kept closed at night.

At all times wardens should set a good example and guard against carelessness.

Fire Preparation

Fire preparation is about familiarising yourself and your residents with what to do in the event of a fire.

The advice given to wardens on this issue varies widely. Some wardens are expected to ensure that their complexes are evacuated should fire break out; others have been advised by their own Fire Officer or by the Fire Brigade not to attempt to clear the building, in view of the fact that, in purpose built schemes, tenants' flats have front doors which are half-hour fire resistant. The view here is that more panic and alarm, together with exposure to smoke and fumes, might result in attempting to evacuate a complex full of frail elderly residents, than would be the case if they stayed in their flats until the fire brigade made the decision as to whom to evacuate.

If you are one of the wardens to whom the latter applies, then it is vital that your tenants are informed and fully understand what to do should they hear the fire alarm sound.

If you are expected to evacuate the building then you should hold fire drills at least twice a year – it helps familiarise tenants with what to do, where the fire exits are, and generally helps them to be prepared should a real emergency occur.

You should keep an up-to-date 'register' of all tenants, plus a list of frail/at risk tenants who would not be able to evacuate their flats in the event of a fire.

If there is no cover on-site for you when you are off duty, you may wish to consider nominating a responsible tenant to call the Fire Brigade if the fire alarm goes off and you are not on the premises.

Some final, general points with regard to fire prevention include ensuring that rubbish is not allowed to build up in communal areas; that nothing is stored in electrical-intake cupboards or boiler rooms, and that fire exits are not obstructed. Lastly, ensure that too many people are not squashed into the common room – you may need to reduce numbers to stay within safety limits. The designated safety officer for your organisation will give you guidance in this area.

Fire Action

Fire Action concerns what to do in the event of a fire. As we have seen, instructions vary as to what you should do, and you should receive clear guidance from your employing organisation regarding evacuation of the building. Whether or not this is the case, your first action should be to call the Fire Brigade by dialling 999, clearly stating the address of the complex. If you discover a fire, set off the fire alarm immediately. Then if at all possible – and without endangering your own safety – try to put out the fire with the appropriate extinguisher. Remember, however, that you are not a trained firefighter.

Ensure you have a list of frail tenants or those unable to leave their flats, to give to the Fire Brigade when they arrive, and ensure access to the complex is clear for the emergency services.

Obviously, all these points can only be general guidelines. You should have clear guidance and instructions from your employing organisation in this area; they will in turn be able to call on the fire brigade for specialist advice, but may not necessarily think to provide this unless you ask. A helpful video on the subject of dealing with fires in sheltered housing schemes – which is useful for tenants as well as wardens since it also discusses fire prevention within tenants' flats – is produced by Austin Charles Associates, called *It could happen – Fire Safety for Sheltered Accommodation.* It could be shown in the common room and used as a basis for stimulating discussion with tenants. It was filmed in a housing association sheltered housing scheme and uses real tenants, not actors, which could provide another focus for discussion, and seems to make it all the more realistic.

Community and Recreational Activities

Introduction

Within their job description, many wardens are given responsibility for encouraging, or in some cases, organising, community activities on their sheltered schemes. There is an assumption here that the facilities are available in order to do so, and as we have seen, the majority of purpose built sheltered complexes have common rooms.

Before simply accepting this as a natural function of the role of the warden and considering some of the ways in which this can be approached, it may help to consider some of the problems associated with this task, together with why it is important, and the ways in which it can benefit the residents.

Many wardens have expressed the view that they are not 'Redcoats' employed to be entertainments manager along with all their other responsibilities; neither is the scheme a holiday camp existing to provide a non-stop selection of entertainers, bingo and coach outings. Others complain that their tenants are too old or too frail or too resistant to joining in to make any community activities a success. Still more point out that, when they have delegated the task of running the social club to a committee of tenants, they have become locked in arguments and internecine warfare, with activities attracting only a chosen few (usually cronies of the committee!) leaving the poor warden as piggy-in-the-middle attempting to keep the peace.

Far from this aspect of the job being the lighter enjoyable side, for many wardens it actually sets up tensions and presents a multitude of problems probably not considered by the original exponents of the principle of sheltered housing built around an integral lounge or common room. Perhaps they had in mind an idyllic picture of home made cakes and Earl Grey tea sipped daintily by white-haired, yet still active, older people, chatting with each other in small, friendly groups dotted around the communal lounge. The warden, naturally, has not made the cakes, or the tea – these are provided, willingly by the tenants. When tea is over, a few tenants exchange farewells and wander back to their flats, whilst others play cards or chess until supper time. As wardens have told us, this type of use of the common room is very rare indeed, and usually exists solely as a fantasy in the minds of those who have very little to do with the running of sheltered housing on a day-to-day basis.

Let us consider some of the reasons why communal activities in sheltered housing schemes can cause problems. Having done so, we can look at the role of the warden in finding some solutions, and at the benefits to be gained by residents if the difficulties can be overcome.

The Sheltered Complex as a Community

The sheltered housing scheme is not a community which has come together by choice; although it is to be hoped that residents have actively chosen to move there, they have not necessarily chosen to be part of one big happy family. They may not want to socialise with other elderly people; they may not have the same interests or tastes in common. In general, their previous lives may not have involved the kind of communal living or participation which often form an integral part of living in a sheltered housing scheme. Whilst for some of the more gregarious residents joining in can be both rewarding and stimulating, for others it can be intimidating.

Given the number of disparate personalities, differences in expectations and needs, and levels of willingness to participate, it is hardly surprising therefore that difficulties with regard to the provision of recreational activities arise. It is possibly also the reason why the old favourite, bingo, is so prevalent; it is the 'safe' option, popular on many sheltered schemes with large numbers of residents and possibly also involving older people living outside the scheme as well.

Activities which attract fewer people than the ubiquitous bingo are sometimes perceived to be unsuccessful. However, there is a strong case for supporting the view that even if only two or three people have participated in, benefited from and enjoyed an activity, then that activity is worthwhile. Success does not have to be measured by the numbers who join in so much as what those who join in have gained by doing so; this concept can sometimes assist wardens to reappraise activities they have formerly perceived to be unsuccessful.

Conflict within the Community

The community itself may be beset with squabbles, divided into factions; or dominated by one or two noisy or bossy members. This is, of course, a reflection of many wider scenarios, particularly involving such groups as tenants associations, political groups, youth clubs – comprising people who have come together with a common interest or purpose yet who seem to detract from their effectiveness by internal arguments. This problem is exacerbated in sheltered housing where the people involved also live in such close proximity to one another.

There are a number of points the warden can consider here, the main one being that conflict is normal, to be expected, and is not the wardens fault! The warden has not failed by 'allowing' a lack of harmony to build up; this would happen in the normal way of things. The advantage of it occurring in a sheltered housing scheme lies in the existence of the warden who, by refusing to take sides, can perhaps enable the conflict to be resolved by using the skills of negotiation and assertiveness, amongst others. (Chapter 4 deals with working with groups in more depth).

Wardens often recount how, having delegated the task of running the social club to a committee, the members of the committee then make a take-over bid for power, excluding the warden, and indeed anyone else who is not part of their particular group. Such experiences have led people to question the validity of delegation, despite agreeing with the principle, since the effects in practice have meant that control of activities continues to reside with a minority.

However, the alternative lies with the warden retaining all the responsibility and all the power which does not accord with the fundamental precept of sheltered housing, which concerns empowering residents to determine their own lives and make their own choices.

Some Creative Solutions

Happily, wardens are resourceful people and have also proposed some constructive ideas for the solution of this dilemma. One idea can be to limit the powers of the committee by a clearly defined constitution. Another involves limiting the length of time the committee members can hold office. A third is to circumvent the committee by organising activities that are different from those of the committee, to appeal to tenants whose needs are not being served, or who are currently excluded. Gradually, responsibility for these can be devolved to the participants. We have found that creative solutions often arise out of treating these issues as a problem solving exercise, where groups exchange ideas for solutions; if you are currently studying for the NWCC you have access to a group with whom you can try this out. If you are not, brainstorming ideas for solutions with a group of colleagues can be both helpful in terms of practical ideas, and in the support you gain through working together on common issues.

Remember too that your manager can also be a valuable resource, since they or close colleagues are likely to have had considerable experience of negotiation with tenant groups. As well as supporting you in your action, they may well have practical advice and assistance to offer.

The Importance of Tenant Participation

Tenant participation is an important aspect of current housing management practice. In a challenging article on how this can be achieved in sheltered housing, 'Participation in Sheltered Housing' (*TPAS News* Spring 1992), Hester Blewitt describes how one local authority is currently developing a Charter of Rights for elderly people living in sheltered schemes, in order to reflect the needs and aspirations of *all* residents. Additionally, she recommends that in order to participate, sheltered scheme tenants need information, resources, and training. In other words, delegation of responsibility cannot take place without the provision of appropriate support. Providing such support can be a legitimate way of the warden remaining involved with what is going on, yet at the same time empowering tenants to make their own choices and decisions about what goes on in the scheme. Hester Blewitt considers the skills needed by the warden in this area are those of 'negotiating, mediating, conciliating and enabling'. Her view is that wardens have a critical role to play in this area, and she comments on how some wardens are providing inspired leadership and encouragement for residents to participate at any level they want, despite the fact that many organisations' recruitment and training policies do not acknowledge the need for such skills.

Increasing Frailty of Tenants

Wardens have often told us of high levels of frailty on their schemes, due to an allocations policy which does not take account of the existing levels of frailty, but is based on 'worst first, due to pressure through demand exceeding supply. This can be a demoralising work situation for a warden – for what if there are no active, sprightly members of the community with whom the community activities can be shared, or to whom tasks can be delegated? Often, wardens exhaust themselves laying on an activity in the common room, doing all the work beforehand, making sure that all the wheelchair bound residents get there – usually pushing the wheelchairs themselves – and doing all the cleaning up afterwards. Such occasions are of necessity few and far between because of the demands they place upon the warden

Some Creative Solutions

When we have considered solutions to this scenario, with groups of wardens, many of them have proposed some interesting and original ways of approaching communal and recreational activities with the very frail. There seems to be a general agreement that the idea of a large activity involving as many people as possible should be abandoned in favour of smaller scale, more individual activities. A creative approach to the use of volunteers, whether through local Age Concern Groups, Volunteer Bureau or schools for example can be adopted, and some of the physical tasks delegated in this way. Because people are physically frail they may be disregarded in terms of the contribution they can make, yet wardens have told us that challenging this assumption has been highly beneficial to all concerned and produced surprising results in terms of the administrative and organisational tasks they have been able to delegate to some more frail residents.

Quality not Quantity – an Example

An example of an activity that illustrated the value of quality rather than quantity and the creative use of volunteers was given by a warden in an oral presentation, following an assignment based on putting into practice a new recreational activity, using volunteers if appropriate, and involving tenants who did not currently participate in such activities. Students were encouraged to extensively consult with residents as to their choices and preferences and match these up with facilities available locally.

This particular sheltered complex had been receiving visits from a local school which had not been going well – the purpose was unclear, the children ended up being noisy and giggly, and everyone was glad when the visits were over. Following consultation with two wheelchair-bound and one blind, though physically able resident, plus discussions with the head of the school and the class teacher, an outing was arranged to a local forest and beauty spot which had good disabled access. Each of the three residents was escorted by two volunteer school pupils, who pushed the wheelchairs, and in the case of the blind resident, described what could be seen along the way. These particular residents had expressed a desire to get out in the fresh air, an opportunity they rarely, if ever, had; this exercise not only met that need, but was the beginning of genuine two-way communication between them and the children, who, rapport having been established, continued to visit them on a one-to-one basis afterwards. This is an inspiring example of creative thought by the warden, and there have been many other such novel ideas and approaches that wardens have recounted to us over the years, proving yet again the resourcefulness of those working in sheltered housing.

Conclusions

Despite the fact that encouraging community activities is not an easy task, it is worthwhile in that it can provide many opportunities for individuals to participate in social events and activities, and in determining what goes on in the scheme. Ultimately, it can help residents to look outwards – events do not have to be limited to residents of the complex only. Older people who do not live in sheltered housing can be invited to participate, thus spreading the benefits of sheltered housing more widely. Social events can be a bridge between the scheme and the outside world; wardens can combine with their colleagues locally to organise joint activities and inter-scheme events.

Finally of course, we must recognise that, just as wardens are not redcoats, the scheme is not a holiday camp. Residents may choose not to join in, and that is their absolute right. Such a choice does not imply any failing on the warden's part, nor should it cause any judgements about the tenant being standoffish. As long as opportunities exist for residents to organise and/or participate in community activities about which they have been fully consulted then the warden has fulfilled yet another aspect of this demanding role.

Settling in New Tenants

It is easy to fall into the trap of assuming that the move into sheltered housing is a positive experience for older people. Whilst we hope of course that it is made through choice, it is, nevertheless, a traumatic experience. If we think back to any experience we have had of being new – first day at a new job or college, or school for example – we can remember how bewildered, and probably apprehensive, we were. Combining these feelings with the stressful and traumatic experience of moving (high on the list of recognised stress factors) we can see that the settling in process for a new tenant is vital in their lives. We can see also that the role of the warden is crucial in making this process work.

Feelings that the New Tenant may Experience

Moving to sheltered housing is probably the last move tenants are likely to make. Whilst they may have looked forward to such a move, many will find that it is also associated with loss – of their old familiar home, surroundings and neighbours. Perhaps they will have had to get rid of furniture as the sheltered flat is smaller than their existing home – where perhaps they may have brought up their family, or lived with their partner. They will be leaving behind associations and memories – no matter that they are moving into a convenient comfortable and secure flat with all the advantages that sheltered housing can give.

Acknowledging such losses and, in doing so, perhaps recognising increased dependency can mean the new tenant must work through a range of feelings including particularly those of fear and inadequacy. These may present as anger, depression or withdrawal, or they may remain hidden, only to manifest themselves at a later stage.

The Range of Skills Used by the Warden

It is clear then that settling in a new tenant uses the warden's range of skills to the full. In particular there will be a need for listening and counselling, helping the new tenant work through the range of feelings in a way which demonstrates the acceptance of such strongly felt emotions. One warden, in writing about this issue, vehemently opposed any attempt to jolly people along, or to provide superficial reassurances; he felt it was vitally important to allow new tenants the space and time to adjust to their new surroundings and come to terms with their feelings. What should be on offer, he felt, was support and time from the warden, plus the knowledge that the new tenant was welcome to participate in the community life of the scheme when they felt ready. (See Chapter 4 for further discussion on counselling skills and loss.)

Practical Tasks

On a practical level when we consider this subject on the certificated course, wardens enjoy working together to produce a list of tasks which need to be carried out when settling in someone new. Although the order and format might vary from one employing organisation to another, wardens have valued the opportunity to discuss the range of tasks, and particularly the timescale over which they should be carried out. The view is always firmly expressed that explanations about the flat, the scheme, the various items of technical equipment, the days social activities take place, the use of the laundry etc., must be spaced out over a period of days if not weeks, since the bewilderment of being new precludes very much being taken in. Written back-up should be given wherever possible, and explanations may need to be repeated many times. Many wardens also offer such creative and welcoming ideas as having a neighbour show the new tenant round the complex so that they know at least one friendly face; and a 'welcome to your New Home' card left in the flat by the warden on the day they move in, often accompanied by a guide to local services and facilities that they may need.

It can be seen therefore that it is through a mixture of an organised, thoughtful approach to the practical and administrative tasks, together with an awareness of the need for the interpersonal skills of listening and counselling, that the warden can enable a new tenant to experience the process of settling in as positively as possible.

Wardens and Their Managers

Introduction

Throughout this chapter we have seen how vital it is for wardens to be given clear guidelines by their employing organisations. It is particularly important for wardens as members of a dispersed workforce to have both a clear understanding of organisational policies in order to present them to those with whom they come into contact, and the confidence to know that support and advice is available when they need it. Clearly, this calls for an understanding on the part of the employer that a particular effort must be made to communicate regularly and clearly with wardens; that although wardens have the capability and skills to work autonomously, they can work most effectively when they are well supported.

Wardens' line managers therefore have a key role to play in this process. They can facilitate greater understanding of the policies and practices of the employing organisation by the warden and they can ensure that the warden is given the necessary tools to carry out the job. Key tasks for the wardens' line manager include regular appraisals, support and guidance on particular issues, and the provision of opportunities for the warden to discuss general aspects of the scheme. Such support not only reduces the feelings of isolation experienced by many wardens but also helps to clarify boundaries. In addition it creates a channel for regular two-way communication. We therefore examine the relationships between wardens and their managers, considering some of the problems and pitfalls and looking at examples of good practice. We look at ways in which wardens themselves can address any problems they may be experiencing in this area.

Finally, we consider the need for each warden to have access to a wardens manual or 'bible' and consider some of the areas which such a handbook might cover.

Who Manages the Warden?

The way in which the warden is managed varies widely between organisations. Some employing authorities – mainly Local Authority Housing Departments – have had a warden's manager or supervisor in post for some years. For others this is a more recent innovation, perhaps stemming from the establishment of a central control alarm system. It is often the case that where there is a specialist wardens' manager who has thought through the needs of a dispersed workforce, there is good communication between wardens and management, including regular wardens meetings, regular support groups and access to training. The need to reduce wardens' isolation and to ensure that, despite not actually working at head office, the warden feels part of the organisation, has been addressed.

Other wardens are supervised by the Housing Officer or Estate Manager – there are many titles for this post, which basically means a housing worker with responsibility for a 'patch' of properties including one or more sheltered schemes. Therefore, the supervision and support of wardens is one of a number of other responsibilities held by the post holder, and their understanding of the role of the warden will vary widely. Sometimes wardens may be managed by the caretaking supervisor. Under these circumstances an overview of the warden service may well be lacking within the organisation, since there is no single person with responsibility for service co-ordination, and as a result there may be little recognition of the specific needs of wardens as a dispersed workforce. Many Local Authorities and Housing Associations still operate in this way.

Wardens Meetings

One common problem experienced by authorities and housing associations that have no co-ordinated approach to the management of the warden service is that, when they call a wardens meeting – usually on an irregular basis and sometimes in response to a crisis – wardens have a number of negative issues to raise, simply because the opportunity to do so is rarely provided. Wardens cope for much of the time as the representatives of their management yet with little or no real understanding of, or identification with, the policies of their employing organisation. Tenants pour out their worries, fears and – frequently – their complaints about the management of the property to the warden who has to take all this on board, frequently being held responsible in the tenants' eyes for the shortcomings of the employing organisation. Small wonder then that wardens use the opportunity of a meeting where a representative of management is present to offload some of this burden, which may have built up over many months; and an unfortunate result of this is that such meetings achieve very little, since managers feel they are being attacked, whilst wardens in turn feel they are not being listened to.

This can lead to a negative cycle, where management call meetings as infrequently as possible in order to avoid the situation just described, whilst in the meantime wardens have little or no opportunity to express their feelings either on an individual or group basis. Hence when the next wardens meeting finally comes round, there is an even greater degree of pent-up frustration to be expressed.

Communication and Support

Of course, there are some shining exceptions to the above situation; a number of wardens with whom we have worked over the years have described excellent structures of support. In such cases, regular individual one-to-one sessions between warden and manager take place, where the manager behaves not in a punitive or judgemental way but acts as a listener and counsellor to the warden. The emphasis here is on the regular sessions, rather than the manager arriving on the scene following a summons because of a crisis. This kind of support is often given in conjunction with regular opportunities for wardens to meet together as a group, both with and without a member of management being present; these meetings may centre around information giving and sharing, or training, or opportunities for feedback. All of these initiatives are major factors in reducing isolation. Additionally the more contact with, and understanding of management that wardens have, the more they will feel part of the organisation, identifying with its policies and practices, and thus able to confidently represent the organisation on the frontline.

Overcoming the Problems

Clearly, then, good support for and communication with wardens brings management enormous benefits, and vice-versa; but for those wardens reading this whose management do not appear to have appreciated this fundamental issue, it may seem somewhat irrelevant, given that you may feel powerless in the face of your management's seeming lack of interest or commitment.

In discussion with wardens over the years about this topic, some initiatives have been suggested which may help those reading this book to move forward on this issue.

One approach is to simply make the direct, and not unreasonable, request to your management for regular meetings.

Research what happens in other areas, and find examples of good practice which you can use to help convince your manager of the need for, and benefits of, regular meetings. When suggesting this to your manager it can also help if you not only provide specific examples but perhaps also give contact names of other wardens' managers who are running successful and constructive meetings themselves.

Some wardens may be working in locations where they are geographically isolated from colleagues – for example within a rural authority with widely scattered schemes, or a housing association without other sheltered complexes in the locality. In such cases there is no immediate local group of colleagues from within the same organisation, but you could consider setting up a local support group of those who work with older people in a variety of settings – home carers, district nurses, carers in Part III accommodation, for example. Such a group can meet regularly, and share approaches, problems and solutions relating to the client group which you all have in common. Chapter 4 can help with setting up a group.

Another possibility might be to slot in to an existing group of wardens working for another organisation. This has been beneficial for some housing association or private sector wardens who have no colleagues from their own organisation in the area yet who meet up with the local authority wardens on a regular basis to discuss issues of mutual benefit.

These are solutions that have worked for some wardens, but they can of course never take the place of regular contact and good communication with your own management. You should, therefore, try to ensure that, even if face-to-face contact is limited between you and your manager, you are kept informed regularly (by post if necessary) of what is happening at head office by being on the circulation list for reports, memos and information items generally.

To get any of these initiatives off the ground, you will need to feel both confident and assertive, so consider the appropriate sections of Chapter 4 before embarking on putting your ideas into practice. You may also wish to discuss them informally with your colleagues. Many wardens have told us that, although denied the opportunity to meet together during working hours they feel it is worthwhile and rewarding to give up some of their leisure time to discuss issues of common interest with their colleagues, perhaps over a meal or drink. Support from colleagues for such initiatives can help with building confidence to make such requests as well as providing supporting evidence to show that others share your views.

The National Wardens Association

Membership of the National Wardens Association (NWA) may help you feel less isolated; their structure of regional groups, together with their national newsletter can provide a comforting reminder that you are not the only warden feeling alone and unsupported; there is a huge network of wardens across the country, and the NWA attempts to link them up, make people aware of the wardens' role – and the problems which wardens face – and generally campaign for improved standards and conditions for wardens. Membership could therefore have a number of spin-offs, including increasing your confidence in your approach to your own management. See the list of useful addresses at the end of the book for how to get in touch with the NWA.

Wardens Manuals

Whether or not wardens have regular communication and support from their line managers, it is important that every warden has a warden's manual – sometimes referred to as a 'Warden's Handbook' or 'Warden's Bible'. This is usually a combination of information regarding the employing organisation's policies and practices in particular areas and specific information regarding that particular scheme.

This is an important document for a number of reasons, the most important being the fact that any member of a dispersed workforce who is unable to easily and informally check procedures with their line manager or colleagues must have a clearly laid down set of criteria to refer to when necessary. It offers protection both to the warden and the employing organisation. Regularly up-dated, it keeps the warden in touch with policies, practices and developments which are formulated at 'head office' yet which are put into practice in the warden's workplace. Devising such a manual, and keeping it current ensures that managers are aware of what the job of the warden actually entails, and if its composition is a joint effort between wardens and management it can greatly enhance understanding on both sides. A manual outlining procedures is an essential element for any organisation wanting to ensure consistent standards of quality.

Naturally every organisation will have its own criteria for what should be included. The headings which follow, therefore are not a prescriptive list, but suggestions only, culled from discussion on this subject over the years with wardens and their managers.

- The organisation – structure and staffing, including contact list; mission statement; rationale or philosophy of sheltered housing provision.
- The role of the warden:
  - job description, job specification and any guidelines and/or policy statement;
  - clarification of areas such as emergencies, first aid, lifting, daily contact (visits, unobtrusive observation, calls on intercom etc.) giving medication etc.;
- Where and how support services for residents can be obtained, e.g. NHS, Social Services, DSS etc.
- Liaison with central control/relief warden/deputy warden.
- What to do in the event of a tenant's death:
  - general procedures;
  - where no Next of Kin exists.
- Master key system, when and how used.
- Repairs – general and emergency.
- Who to contact during out-of-hours emergencies.
- The various alarm systems/call systems in use on the sheltered complex.
- Administrative procedures required by the employing organisation, e.g. petty cash, stores, ordering, guest room, TV licences etc.
- Tenants' records – procedures and practices, access etc.
- Responsibility with regard to premises including health and safety duties and responsibilities.
- Fire prevention/fire safety.
- Food Hygiene.
- Settling in new tenants – guidelines and checklist.
- Monitoring of gardening, cleaning, window cleaning, other contractors etc.
- Useful addresses:
  - Contractors for servicing and inspection of equipment;
  - Social/recreational contacts;
  - GPs, clinics, local hospitals, district nursing services, social services department;
  - voluntary organisations
  - other local sheltered schemes etc., etc.

However well thought out and comprehensive any warden's manual is, it should not be considered a substitute for support and face-to-face contact with the warden's line manager.

Rather, it is part of the communication which exists between management and the warden, another element in the support and on-going training which, we believe, all wardens should be receiving on a regular basis.

Code of Practice for Wardens

A code of practice (see Figure 7.1) for wardens and other workers in sheltered housing has recently been proposed by the Centre for Sheltered Housing Studies, an educational charity providing training courses for wardens. This code is designed to provide a framework within which wardens can carry out their jobs effectively, providing a common set of values and expectations, thus benefiting wardens, their employers and residents alike. The idea of the code has been supported and sponsored by a number of national organisations which represent the sheltered housing service, including the National Wardens Association, the Institute of Housing, the National Federation of Housing Associations, Age Concern and Help the Aged.

The working party which produced the code intends it to be of value in the following ways:

- To provide wardens, resident managers and others working in sheltered housing with a common point of reference on the values, attitudes, legal understanding and aspects of practical action which are generally accepted as representing good practice in sheltered housing management.
- To encourage and support providers and employers to define clear policies for the management of sheltered housing and to provide staff with positive reporting lines and clear job descriptions.
- To assist providers of sheltered housing to define clearly for residents the services that they may expect and to identify the rights and responsibilities of residents as owners, tenants or licensees and as members of a sheltered housing community.
- To encourage and support employers to offer appropriate training for wardens and others and to encourage wardens to accept and act on a responsibility for their own self-development.

Code of practice
for wardens and other workers in sheltered housing

1. To offer equal opportunity and fair treatment to all residents without discrimination on account of race, gender, disability, religion, age or sexual orientation.
2. To recognise, respect and safeguard the individuality and personal rights of each resident whilst acknowledging the responsibilities to others.
3. To understand and respect the confidentiality of knowledge and information relating to individual residents and the employer.
4. To facilitate independence and the well-being of residents both as individuals and within the group as a whole.
5. To be sensitive and impartial in the delivery of services.
6. To act always with honesty and integrity.
7. To ensure that professional responsibility is never sacrificed for personal interest.
8. To establish and maintain high standards of personal conduct and professional relationships.
9. To acknowledge the need for continuing professional training and self-development.
10. To ensure that internal procedures relating to statutory obligations of the employer are understood and implemented.
11. To understand the role of other service providers and significant people in the lives of residents and be committed to working effectively with them.
12. To be aware of and to accept, a responsibility to contribute to the setting of objectives, policies and procedures of the employer.

FIGURE 7.1

References and Further Reading

Austin Charles Associates (1991) video – *It could happen – Fire Safety for Sheltered Accommodation* Austin Charles Associates.
Blewitt H (1992) Participation in Sheltered Housing *TPAS News* Spring 1992, p 5.

LOOKING AHEAD

Sheltered housing and those who work in it have suffered from unclear goals and a changing political and economic climate. In particular, changing demographic and community care policies have all but extinguished the original concept of a good neighbour type of warden 'keeping an eye' on reasonably fit tenants. The warden's role, never terribly clear, is now even more problematic for the post holder, for tenants and families, for management and for other agencies as we explored in depth in Chapter 1.

We have tried, in this book, to give an account of these changes that have affected our readers so extensively. As importantly we have also teased out the essential skills used by wardens in their work and offered them ideas and tools for coping with these changes and the pressures they are under.

We hope the ideas and information we have offered have been useful to wardens of all kinds especially those considering or already studying for the National Wardens Certificate Course (NWCC).

Our aims have been to stimulate thought, validate existing skills and knowledge and provoke further enquiry. Many of our students have gained such confidence and enthusiasm for learning that they have continued their education and training after the course has finished, perhaps through reading more or perhaps through in-service courses offered by their employers. Housing organisations have in the past invested heavily in the bricks and mortar of housing but not in the staff paid to work with the people living in these properties. Training housing workers in relevant aspects of customer care, management, budgeting and so on is now seen in theory as of great importance to the overall effectiveness of housing organisations. Sadly the current economic climate has yet again led to cuts in training budgets in some agencies. Sometimes, however, cuts can lower people's expectations and lead them not to ask for training. It is always worth ensuring you are well informed of available courses by going on the mailing list of relevant organisations (e.g. Age Concern) and asking whether funds are available. Some agencies operate stop/go policies on training and there is always a chance that your application could arrive in a 'go' period. For most wardens the motto 'if you don't ask, you won't get' is very true of training – so ask!

Another avenue for meeting training and education needs is to enrol at a local college for a short course on say Assertiveness,

Counselling, Stress Management, Report Writing skills, perhaps paying for this yourself.

Alternatively you could, after the NWCC, go on to take the Advanced Certificate Course for wardens now being run at several colleges throughout the country, where students are encouraged to take responsibility for their own self-directed learning. Alternative further education includes the BTEC Higher National Certificate in Housing, the IOH Professional Diploma or a career move into social work. Ask for prospectuses from all your local colleges and write to the specialist professional bodies listed at the end of this chapter under useful addresses.

Another aspect to the training possibilities that will be available in the early 1990s for wardens will be the NVQ dimension. Briefly, NVQs – National Vocational Qualifications – will enable individuals and training managers to target *specific* skills required within their work; people's existing capabilities will be recognised as well as their requirements for further training. It is anticipated that NVQs relevant to wardens will be in operation by the mid-1990s. NVQs should allow the warden a significant degree of flexibility in gaining further development, as well as in recognising existing achievements.

We hope that this book has opened up or enhanced opportunities for you to continue your own personal and professional development. The role of the warden is continuing to change, and it is time for wardens themselves, individually and collectively, to take the lead in this initiative. We hope this book will play its part in stimulating thought and debate, but at the end of the day it is you, the warden, who is the most important person in this process.

Useful Addresses

Age Concern England
Astral House
1268 London Road
London SW16 4EJ
(will send a full list of publications)

Age Exchange Reminiscence Centre
11 Blackheath Village
London SE3 9LA

The Alzheimer's Disease Society
158–160 Balham High Road
London SW12 9BN

British Association for Counselling
37a Sheep Street
Rugby
Warwickshire CV21 3BX

British Association of Social Workers
16 Kent Street
Birmingham B5 6RD

British Medical Association (BMA)
Family Doctor Publications
Tavistock Square
London WC1B 9JR

BTEC
Central House
Upper Woburn Place
London WC1H 0HH

Carers National Association
29 Chilworth Mews
London W2 3RG

Central Council for Training and Education in Social Work
(CCETSW)
Derbyshire House
St Chad's Street
WC1H 8AD
(for information on training as a social worker)

Centre for Policy on Ageing
15–31 Ironmonger Row
London EC1V 3QP
(publishing address to order their books:

Bailey Bros Distribution Ltd
Learoyd Road
Mountfield Industrial Estate
New Romney
Kent TN28 8XU)

Centre for Sheltered Housing Studies
Dog Lane Mews
Dog Lane
Bewdley DU12 2EF

Council for Care for the Elderly
Tyman House
Bonny Street
London NW1 9LR

CRUSE (Bereavement Care)
Cruse House
126 Sheen Road
Richmond
Surrey TW9 1UR

Disabled Living Foundation (DLF)
380–384 Harrow Road
London W9 2HU

Equal Opportunities Commission
Overseas House
Manchester M3 3HN

Ethnic Communities Oral History Project
2 Royal Parade
Dawes Road
London SW6 7RE

Help the Aged
St James's Walk
London EC1R 0BE

HERA for Women (Housing Employment Register and Advice)
4th Floor
2 Valentine Place
London SE1 8QH

Institute of Housing
Octavia House
Westwood Business Park
Westwood Way
Coventry CV4 8JP

Institute of Race Relations
2–6 Leeke Street
London WC1X 9HS

National Council for Voluntary Organisations
26 Bedford Square
London WC1B 3HU

National Extension College
18 Brookland Avenue
Cambridge CB2 2HN
(regarding Distance Learning)

National Federation of Housing Associations
175 Gray's Inn Road
London WC1X 8UP

National Wardens Association
c/o Anne Flynn
20 Vale Court
93 Bulwer Road
New Barnet
Herts EN5 5EZ

The Open College
Freepost TK 1006
Brentford
Middlesex TW8 8BR

The Open University
Milton Keynes MK7 6DH
(regarding Distance Learning)

Parry Thompson Associates
5 Glenmire Terrace
Stanstead Abbotts
Ware
Herts SG12 8AD

Pensioners Link
405–407 Holloway Road
London N7 6HJ

Pensioners Voice (National Federation of Retirement Pensions Associations)
Melling House
14 St Peter Street
Blackburn
Lancs BB2 2HD

Royal National Institute for the Blind
(RNIB)
224–228 Great Portland Street
London W1N 6AA

Royal National Institute for the Deaf
(RNID)
105 Gower Street
London WC1

SPOD (Association to Aid the Sexual and Personal Relationships of people with a Disability)
286 Camden Road
London N7 0BJ

University of the Third Age (U3A)
1 Stockwell Green
London SW9 9JF

Winslow Press
Freepost
Bicester
Oxon OX6 OBR
(for training, reminiscence, and other materials. Free Catalogue)

INDEX